Internment of Japanese Americans

Other titles in the World History Series

Internment of Japanese Americans

John F. Wukovits

LUCENT BOOKS
A part of Gale, Cengage Learning

Detroit • New York • San Francisco • New Haven, Conn • Waterville, Maine • London

GALE
CENGAGE Learning·

LIBRARY OF CONGRESS CATALOGING-IN-PUBLICATION DATA

Wukovits, John F., 1944-
  Internment of Japanese Americans / by John F. Wukovits.
    p. cm. -- (World history)
  Includes bibliographical references and index.
  ISBN 978-1-4205-0824-6 (hardcover)
  1. Japanese Americans--Evacuation and relocation, 1942-1945. 2. World War, 1939-1945--Japanese Americans. 3. Japanese--United States--History. I. Title.
  D769.8.A6W85 2012
  940.53'1773--dc23
                                                                2012021422

Lucent Books
27500 Drake Rd.
Farmington Hills, MI 48331

ISBN-13: 978-1-4205-0824-6
ISBN-10: 1-4205-0824-5

Printed in the United States of America
1 2 3 4 5 6 7 16 15 14 13 12

Contents

Foreword

Each year, on the first day of school, nearly every history teacher faces the task of explaining why his or her students should study history. Many reasons have been given. One is that lessons exist in the past from which contemporary society can benefit and learn. Another is that exploration of the past allows us to see the origins of our customs, ideas, and institutions. Concepts such as democracy, ethnic conflict, or even things as trivial as fashion or mores, have historical roots.

Reasons such as these impress few students, however. If anything, these explanations seem remote and dull to young minds. Yet history is anything but dull. And therein lies what is perhaps the most compelling reason for studying history: History is filled with great stories. The classic themes of literature and drama—love and sacrifice, hatred and revenge, injustice and betrayal, adversity and overcoming adversity—fill the pages of history books, feeding the imagination as well as any of the great works of fiction do.

The story of the Children's Crusade, for example, is one of the most tragic in history. In 1212 Crusader fever hit Europe. A call went out from the pope that all good Christians should journey to Jerusalem to drive out the hated Muslims and return the city to Christian control. Heeding the call, thousands of children made the journey. Parents bravely allowed many children to go, and entire communities were inspired by the faith of these small Crusaders. Unfortunately, many boarded ships were captained by slave traders, who enthusiastically sold the children into slavery as soon as they arrived at their destination. Thousands died from disease, exposure, and starvation on the long march across Europe to the Mediterranean Sea. Others perished at sea.

Another story, from a modern and more familiar place, offers a soul-wrenching view of personal humiliation but also the ability to rise above it. Hatsuye Egami was one of 110,000 Japanese Americans sent to internment camps during World War II. "Since yesterday we Japanese have ceased to be human beings," he wrote in his diary. "We are numbers. We are no longer Egamis, but the number 23324. A tag with that number is on every trunk, suitcase and bag. Tags, also, on our breasts." Despite such dehumanizing treatment, most internees worked hard to control their bitterness. They created workable communities inside the camps and demonstrated again and again their loyalty as Americans.

These are but two of the many stories from history that can be found in the pages of the Lucent Books World History series. All World History titles rely on sound research and verifiable evidence, and all give students a clear sense of time, place, and chronology through maps and timelines as well as text.

All titles include a wide range of authoritative perspectives that demonstrate the complexity of historical interpretation and sharpen the reader's critical thinking skills. Formally documented quotations and annotated bibliographies enable students to locate and evaluate sources, often instantaneously via the Internet, and serve as valuable tools for further research and debate.

Finally, Lucent's World History titles present rousing good stories, featuring vivid primary source quotations drawn from unique, sometimes obscure sources such as diaries, public records, and contemporary chronicles. In this way, the voices of participants and witnesses as well as important biographers and historians bring the study of history to life. As we are caught up in the lives of others, we are reminded that we too are characters in the ongoing human saga, and we are better prepared for our own roles.

Important Dates at the Time of the

1860–1935
Approximately 135,000 Japanese move from Japan to the United States, most settling along the West Coast.

1906
The Board of Education for San Francisco, California, segregates Japanese American children.

1933
Franklin D. Roosevelt becomes president of the United States.

1943
In January the U.S. government announces it will form an all-Nisei army combat unit.

In February teams of government personnel administer the loyalty questionnaire to interned Japanese Americans.

In June the U.S. Supreme Court finds for the U.S. government in *Hirabayashi v. United States*.

1900	1910	1920	1930	1940

1917–1918
The United States fights in World War I.

1941
On December 7 Japan attacks Pearl Harbor in Hawaii.

1942
In February President Roosevelt issues Executive Order 9066.

In March President Roosevelt creates the War Relocation Authority (WRA).

From March to October the U.S. government relocates Japanese Americans from the West Coast to assembly centers.

In May Japanese American Gordon K. Hirabayashi, a student at the University of Washington, files a lawsuit to halt the Japanese American evacuation.

In June the U.S. Navy defeats the Imperial Japanese Navy in the Battle of Midway.

During the summer and fall, the U.S. government allows Japanese Americans to leave the internment camps to help harvest crops or to attend college.

In December rioting erupts in Manzanar.

Internment of Japanese Americans

1944

In June Allied forces land at Normandy in France to begin their mainland assault against Germany.

In December the U.S. Supreme Court finds for the government in *Korematsu v. United States*; in *Ex Parte Endo* the Court rules the government can no longer detain Japanese American Mitsuye Endo as a military threat; President Roosevelt announces that beginning January 2, 1945, Japanese Americans can return to their homes.

1946

Tule Lake internment camp closes.

1976

President Gerald Ford officially rescinds Executive Order 9066.

1945   1955   1965   1975   1985

1945

In August the United States drops atomic bombs on the Japanese cities of Hiroshima and Nagasaki, and Japan surrenders.

In September the Japanese sign the document of surrender, officially ending World War II.

In December the U.S. government closes nine internment camps.

1983

Attorney Peter Irons successfully files suit to have the wartime convictions of Japanese Americans Fred T. Korematsu and Gordon K. Hirabayashi overturned.

1988

President Ronald Reagan signs a bill providing for letters of apology and twenty thousand dollars to each survivor of the internment.

Introduction

Altered Lives

On December 7, 1941, Japan attacked the U.S. military forces stationed at Pearl Harbor in Hawaii, drawing the United States into World War II, a war that had been raging in Europe since 1939. Life in America changed forever after that day. Young men left to fight in the war, and families faced rationing of food and supplies, while worrying about their young men and the progress of the war. People wondered how the war would affect world society and whether those nations who commanded power and respect in 1941 would hold similar positions when the guns quieted. This time in U.S. history was very similar to the period following the September 11, 2001, terrorist attack on the United States, when nineteen men hijacked four airliners and crashed them into the World Trade Center in New York, the Pentagon in Virginia, and a field in Pennsylvania. After both the Pearl Harbor and September 11th attacks, citizens of the United States entered an uncertain world, one in which the customs and ways of life changed dramatically.

Even after World War II ended in 1945, uncertainty continued as a new world order, dominated by the democratic United States on one side of the Atlantic Ocean and the Communist Soviet Union on the other, began. The end of the war did at least allow people to return to their former occupations. Careers resumed, schooling continued, and old friendships picked up where they left off. Families welcomed back their returning soldiers, each of whom replaced their army khaki or navy blue uniforms with the latest civilian apparel. Residents of large cities and small towns realized that few things remained the same as they had been before December 7, 1941, but they had each other, and at least some aspects offered a comforting familiarity—the small corner drugstore and gasoline station serviced the same neighborhoods; churches comforted long-standing congregations; and the milkman still delivered milk and fresh products directly to people's homes.

Japanese Americans, however, faced more uncertainty and unfamiliarity, for their lives had been irrevocably altered by a federal government program that ripped them from their homes and imprisoned them during the war in places that some historians condemn as concentration camps. Fearful of spies and another surprise attack, the U.S. government forced more than 110,000 Japanese Americans to leave behind homes, businesses, friends, and occupations and spend much of the war behind walls topped with barbed wire and guarded by rifle-wielding soldiers, despite the fact that many of them were born in the United States and were American citizens. They had committed no crime, appeared in no court, and convicted by no jury. Their only offense was that they were of Japanese descent; they looked like the enemy who had attacked Pearl Harbor and inflicted grievous damage to U.S. forces in the Pacific.

"This was a bleak period in the history of American freedom," wrote noted author James A. Michener in 1976. "A few isolated voices tried to protest—some

Japanese-American families were evacuated from their homes in California and sent to the Manzanar internment camp. Life at the camp was very different from what they were used to, and these experiences have had long-lasting effects for all who were there.

clergymen, some scholars, some members of the government, a surprising number of military personnel who knew the Japanese Americans and understood the true situation—but our nation was bent on revenge."[1]

John Y. Tateishi, who at age three was evacuated along with his parents from his Los Angeles, California, home and placed in the Manzanar internment camp in eastern California, felt the effects firsthand. He writes,

> For us, the summer of '42 was a time of confusion and fear, and a time of lost innocence. There were no tree-lined streets in our world as we suddenly found ourselves in prisons in the middle of deserts, displaced and bewildered outcasts in our own country. We clung to our parents, trusting that they would protect us from what we could not possibly understand. We looked up at guard towers and felt a deep fear of armed soldiers who stood guard over us, and felt within our hearts the meaning of barbed-wire fences which, for us, was a symbol of a new America.[2]

When the war was over, other citizens reveled in their nation's victory and returned to family, friends, and occupations, but Japanese Americans like Tateishi were left to pick up the pieces of shattered lives. A few fortunate families were able to return to their jobs and to their houses, which had been tended to by friendly neighbors in their absence, but most had to begin anew in a society that, during wartime, had turned its back on them.

As Tateishi writes, the war years were "not for us what it was for the rest of America's children. While the rest of America remembers those years of World War II with a sense of pride and nostalgia for a glorious past, for us, the kids of the camps, the experience was very, very different."[3]

Any Japanese American, no matter the age or gender, would have said the same. Young and old, male and female—all suffered indignities during the war because, citizen or not, born in the country or not, they looked like the enemy and shared a cultural link to the enemy. That experience shattered their lives during the war and affected them deeply in the years following.

Chapter One

Background to Evacuation

Japan is an island nation, which means there are limited opportunities for a growing population. Valuable parcels of farmland pass from generation to generation in the same family, leaving few options to those who lack ownership. In the years prior to World War II, some Japanese found a solution. They left their country for the United States, where plentiful land increased the prospects for possessing a farm. Others came to the United States seeking better-paying jobs in a variety of occupations, including fishing. Between 1860 and 1935, approximately 135,000 Japanese left their homeland to live in the United States, with almost 100,000 settling in California.

The New Immigrants

Many Japanese immigrants soon found themselves in the midst of other predicaments. Some Americans resented the presence of Japanese immigrants, because they not only took valuable farmland, but they were also willing to work for lower pay.

In the face of growing hostility, Japanese immigrants turned to each other for solace and held tightly to the customs they grew up with in Japan. They continued to speak Japanese, formed social clubs, set up institutions to take care of their own poor, and celebrated Japanese holidays. At the same time, they considered themselves residents of the United States and pledged to follow the nation's laws. This first generation of Japanese Americans is known as Issei.

The sons and daughters of the Issei who were born in the United States more readily blended in with American society. Having been born in the United States, they were automatically citizens of the nation, and not having grown up in Japan, they lacked direct ties with the older country and considered themselves 100 percent American.

A ship of Japanese immigrants arrives in San Francisco. Japanese immigrants continued to practice their customs in the United States, but their children adopted more American traits and practices.

They respected their parents' cultural ways but longed to bring more American influence and customs into their lives. This second generation of Japanese Americans, known as Nisei, lived in two cultures, the one offered by their parents and the one they encountered every day outside the home.

Born in Vashon Island, Washington, in 1925, Mary Matsuda Gruenewald typified the Nisei, or second-generation Japanese American. Her father came to the United States in 1898 and settled on Vashon Island, where he cultivated strawberry fields. He and his wife spoke Japanese and maintained Japanese customs in the home but insisted that their children attend local schools, learn English, and develop friendships.

Gruenewald enjoyed a normal childhood amidst affable neighbors. Her parents emphasized the importance of being a loyal citizen and told Gruenewald that the United States offered opportunity and equality to all. At the same time, they stressed values passed to them by their parents in Japan, such as the importance of family, courtesy and respect for others, humility, the value of hard work, and that their behavior reflected on the family. For much of her early life Gruenewald inhabited two worlds—one outside the home, where she came into frequent contact with American customs, and one inside the home, where Japanese customs remained strong.

Other Americans saw little difference between the Issei and Nisei. Unlike the sons and daughters of European immigrants, who tended to look more like the mainstream American citizen and thus more readily blended in, Asians from Japan, China, and other nations on the far side of the Pacific had a distinctive appearance. As the *New York Times* concluded in 1935, the Nisei "are American by birth but Japanese by appearance." As citizens they enjoyed rights that their parents, who had not been born in the United States, did not, but they faced their own issues, "for not only are they not accepted by the white Americans around them but they are far removed from the native Japanese, as those who return to Japan soon discover."[4]

A Long History of Discrimination

Discrimination against Asians dates back to the American Civil War (1861–1865), when Chinese immigrants helped construct the intercontinental railroad that connected the East and West Coasts. When the project ended in 1869, most Chinese resettled near San Francisco, California, drawing the wrath of white Americans who were uncomfortable with the presence of such a large influx of Asians.

In 1882 opposition to Chinese immigrants led the U.S. Congress to pass the Chinese Exclusion Act, which banned further immigration from China for ten years. The act was extended for another decade in 1892, and subsequent extensions kept the act in force for another fifty years. California, housing the largest community of Asians in the nation, into the twentieth century excluded them from certain places such as swimming pools, and banned marriage between white Americans and people of Asian descent.

"The Chinese and Japanese are not bona fide citizens," declared San Francisco mayor James Phelan in 1900. "They are not the stuff of which American citizens can be made. . . . Personally we have nothing against the Japanese, but as they will not assimilate with us and their social life is so different from ours, let them keep a respectful distance."[5]

Bitterness increased later that same year when bubonic plague swept through the San Francisco population. When investigators traced the outbreak to rats that had crossed the Pacific aboard ships from Asia, some citizens blamed the subsequent deaths on their Asian neighbors.

In 1905 the *San Francisco Chronicle*, the most influential newspaper on the West Coast, started a long-running series of articles about the "problem" of Asian immigrants Almost every day for months, the paper ran articles depicting the turmoil brought to the area by Asian immigrants, focusing its efforts mainly on Japanese Americans. That same year saw the formation of the Japanese and Korean Exclusion League, an organization devoted to banning further immigration from those two nations.

Japanese Americans responded by forming the Japanese Association of America, an organization that gave legal advice and information on welfare and other social issues to persons of Japanese descent. It raised money to combat anti-Japanese sentiment, hoping that educating white Americans about Japanese immigrants might reduce discrimination.

Tensions flared in 1906 when the San Francisco Board of Education removed ninety-three Japanese American children

Japanese Everywhere

In the early months of 1942, California attorney general Earl Warren claimed that Japanese agents and spies had infiltrated numerous locations in the state. He had no proof, but his statements fostered suspicion of Japanese Americans and helped justify the actions taken to remove them from their homes. To bolster his contentions, Warren listed a few examples:

Japs adjacent to new Livermore Military Airport.

Japs adjacent to Southern Pacific and Western Pacific Railroads.

Japs in vicinity of Oakland Airport.

Japs in vicinity to Holt Caterpillar Tractor Co., San Leandro.

Japs adjacent to all dams supplying water to San Diego and vicinity.

Japs adjacent to all power lines supplying the city of San Diego and vicinity.

Quoted in Michi Nishiura Weglyn. *Years of Infamy: The Untold Story of America's Concentration Camps*. New York: Morrow, 1976, pp. 37–38.

A Chinese railroad worker labors on the Central Pacific Railroad in the 1860s. The influx of Asians to the United States made white citizens uncomfortable and led to the passage of the Chinese Exclusion Act.

from twenty schools and placed them in a segregated school for Asians. The Japanese government vehemently objected to what it considered an outrage against people of Japanese origin, and anti-American riots erupted in Japan.

U.S. president Theodore Roosevelt tried to calm matters by criticizing the board's actions and by opening lines of communications with the Japanese government. In a series of notes passed between Roosevelt and Japan's leaders, Japan agreed to stop issuing passports for laborers to immigrate to the United States, where they competed with white Americans for jobs, while Roosevelt promised to combat anti-Japanese laws wherever they appeared.

Roosevelt's intercession failed to halt anti-Japanese measures, however. In 1913 California's legislators passed the Alien Land Bill, which prevented Japanese Americans who were not citizens from owning farmland. Eleven years later Congress passed the Immigration Act of 1924, banning further immigration from Japan and blocking Issei from becoming citizens.

Japan vigorously protested what it considered unfair treatment of Japanese nationals. A prominent Japanese newspaper, *Yorozu*, said of the Alien Land Bill, "May 26 [the day the measure passed] should be remembered as a day of national humiliation for Japanese. We must organize a nationwide movement against America. In the remotest hamlets we must make known that Americans are unworthy of our friendship. We are partly to blame for the present situation. We have trusted America to an unwarranted extent."[6]

Hard Feelings Intensify

In the 1930s Japan increased its military might, which alarmed some nations, including the United States. Japan's desire to expand outside its borders made other Pacific countries, such as China and the Philippines, nervous. In the United States, sentiment toward Japanese Americans hardened each time Japan grabbed headlines, especially in the early 1930s when Japan invaded Manchuria and brutally subjected the populace. People boycotted stores owned by Japanese Americans, and fifteen hundred Arizona farmers, holding banners proclaiming,

"get out or be put out,"[7] marched near Phoenix, Arizona, to demonstrate against the presence of Japanese American farmers in their valley.

Mary Tsukamoto, born in San Francisco to Japanese parents, recalled her white American high school classmates taunting Japanese American students, in some cases even physically assaulting them, because of Japanese atrocities in Manchuria. Bitterness grew in 1940 when the Japanese government signed an agreement with Nazi Germany and Fascist Italy to provide mutual support for each other over the next decade.

By 1940, just over one hundred thousand people of Japanese ancestry lived in the three West Coast states of California, Oregon, and Washington. Most Nisei had never been to Japan, but their parents maintained ties with the mother country.

Despite affection for Japan, loyalty to the United States was an accepted sentiment in the Japanese American community. They had left Japan seeking better opportunities, and they gave their loyalty to the nation that offered them an improved life. They considered themselves no different than the immigrants who crossed the Atlantic Ocean from England, Ireland, Germany, and Italy. Shortly before World War II erupted, Japanese American Helen Mineta, a secretary at San Jose State College in California, chatted with her friends about what she would do if war with Japan became a reality. "It won't concern me," she quickly replied, "because I'm an American!"[8]

Certain government agencies agreed, as surveillance reports of the Japanese American communities on the West Coast submitted in 1940 and 1941 from the Office of Naval Intelligence and the Federal Bureau of Investigation (FBI) proved. The reports concluded there was no basis for the contentions that Japanese Americans would turn against the United States and sabotage military installations once war with Japan was declared and stated that the vast majority of Japanese Americans held a deep attachment to the United States. A government agent hired a safecracker to break in to the Japanese consulate in Los Angeles and retrieve documents from the office's safe. The documents divulged that Japanese consular officials distrusted Japanese Americans and equated them to traitors. Since the U.S. government kept these reports secret, however, the public and local politicians later acted on unfounded assumptions, which helped produce more hysteria and discrimination.

Feelings against Japanese immigrants in the United States hardened after Japan's government signed an agreement with Benito Mussolini of Italy (left) and Adolf Hitler of Germany (right) in 1940.

Even Eleanor Roosevelt, the wife of President Franklin D. Roosevelt sided with Japanese Americans. Shortly before the war she wrote an article that appeared in the *New York Times* stating that should the nation go to war, no one should be concerned over losing his or her rights because of their country of origin. "This is equally applicable to the Japanese who cannot become citizens but have lived here for thirty or forty years and to those newcomers [refugees from Nazi Germany] who have not yet had time to become citizens."[9]

Roosevelt's appeal to fair play landed on deaf ears on the West Coast, where citizens were concerned with the large presence of Japanese Americans. "Yet, in California opinion, it is impossible to speak of the Japanese without considering them as a problem," wrote a reporter covering the situation for the *New York Times*. "The Californian bristles at the mention of them; and not only the native-born Californian. The thousands of newcomers who never saw a Japanese in their home towns in Iowa or Kansas soon pick up the habit. It is part of the atmosphere, like the conversation about the climate." The reporter added that much of the bitterness resulted not because of who the Japanese Americans were, but how they looked. Unlike immigrants from Germany and Italy, whose facial structure and skin color allowed them to blend in with mainstream society, the Japanese Americans could not physically blend in. "The children of Europe-an nationalities look like the composite American; the children of the Japanese can never change their appearance, no matter how American their accent or slangy their speech."[10]

The Day the War Started for America

On the morning of December 7, 1941, Tsukamoto and Gruenewald had no idea that their world would so dramatically change before supper. Tsukamoto was attending church that Sunday morning when her husband rushed in with the news that Japanese aircraft had just bombed Pearl Harbor. "I remember how stunned we were," she later recalled of that transformative moment. "And suddenly the whole world turned dark. We started to speak in whispers, and because of our experience in Florin [her California home city, where she had endured anti-Japanese sentiment], we immediately sensed something terrible was going to happen."[11]

Gruenewald had just returned home from the Vashon Methodist Church, fully expecting another typical Sunday that mixed work on the family's strawberry farm with a bounteous family dinner. "It was my last carefree morning preoccupied with all the trivial cares and worries of a sixteen-year-old American teenager. It was also the last time I fully believed I was an American." Gruenewald knew that something was amiss the moment she walked into the family home. Her father, who would normally then be laboring in the fields, sat at kitchen table, eyes down, silent.

Different Generations

In Japanese there are three words that identify the different generations of Japanese Americans: *Issei*, *Nisei*, and *Sansei*. Issei are native Japanese who immigrated to the United States, mostly in the early decades of the twentieth century. Issei are first-generation Japanese Americans.

Nisei are the children born in the United States to Issei parents. Since they were born in the country, they automatically became citizens by law. Nisei are second-generation Japanese Americans.

Sansei are third-generation Japanese Americans, most of whom were born after World War II.

Her mother stared out the window, her pale face matching the white of the table linen. As Gruenewald's father told her that Japan had started a war with the United States, his head dropped and his shoulders slumped, as if he had just suffered a catastrophic loss. "Now I had a gnawing feeling of guilt—guilt for being Japanese," Gruenewald later wrote. "I didn't want to think about the possibility that now American people would consider me as the enemy."[12]

Larry Tajiri, a Japanese American newspaperman, walked through Times Square in New York City that momentous day. He felt assaulted by Japan's attack on the United States, just as most other Americans, and wanted to do something. He also knew that he would experience the war years somewhat differently than most American citizens would. "We may have been a little ashamed of our faces as we walked through those crowded New York streets on that December night," he wrote. "We are Americans by every right, birth, education and belief, but our faces are those of the enemy."[13]

Japanese Americans attempted to reassure their countrymen that they were as loyal to the nation as anyone else. Saburo Kido, president of the Japanese American Citizens League (JACL), the most prominent organization promoting the interests of Americans of Japanese descent, sent a telegram to President Roosevelt in Pearl Harbor's aftermath stating that "Japanese Americans are stunned and horrified at this morning's unwarranted attack by Japan upon American soil, our country. We want to convey to you that we unequivocally condemn Japan for this unprecedented breach of good faith." Kido promised that the JACL would do everything possible to aid in "the defense of our land against this attack," pledged "our fullest cooperation to you, Mr. President, and

A U.S. ship explodes during the Japanese attack on Pearl Harbor in 1941. The United States quickly declared war on Japan in response to the surprise attack. Although Japanese American citizens were also upset at the attack, they faced suspicion and discrimination from other Americans.

to our country," and vowed "to expend every effort to repel this invasion together with our fellow Americans."[14] Actions backed Kido's words. In Seattle, Washington, two hundred Japanese Americans volunteered for civil defense work.

Despite those efforts, Japanese Americans faced uncertainty and doubt in the days following Pearl Harbor. On December 8 Yamato Ichihashi, one of Stanford University's most revered history professors, looked through the open door of his classroom before entering and asked his students if he should walk in. They welcomed the popular Ichihashi with wild applause. That same Monday morning every teacher and student treated Gruenewald with kindness, but she wondered if those actions masked deeper, harsher emotions. "I am an American girl yet I don't look like one," she recalled. "I am Japanese but ashamed that I am."[15] In some indefinable way, over the weekend she had become an outsider.

Elsewhere, other Japanese Americans experienced the hatred that Gruenewald feared. In San Carlos, California, someone threw a rock through the window of a gas station and fruit stand owned by Robert and Teiko Wada, and most of their white customers took their business to other establishments. In Seattle workers for the Northern Pacific Railroad threatened to quit unless management fired the handful of Japanese American laborers, and twenty-six Nisei resigned when people demanded they leave their posts at the city's public schools. One county hospital fired a Japanese American brain surgeon, and some patients refused to be treated by Japanese American nurses.

Within twenty-four hours of the attack on Pearl Harbor, the Justice and War Departments ordered the arrests of certain enemy aliens who resided on the West Coast. Enemy aliens are people who live in the United States, are not U.S. citizens, and are still citizens of a country that is at war with or has attacked the United States. The FBI gathered teachers, Buddhist priests, and other prominent individuals in the Japanese American community, as well as some German and Italian Americans, then assured the public that the coast was secure from enemy spies and saboteurs. Japanese Americans had to hand over their cameras, which government officials explained might be used to take photos of American military installations, and their guns.

Rumors Worsen Matters

People on the West Coast felt vulnerable to attack not only because they resided closest to the Japanese enemy, but also because the region housed many valuable aircraft factories. A vast aircraft complex belonging to the Boeing Company lay near Seattle, and North American Aviation and Lockheed Aircraft Company operated aircraft plants near Los Angeles. They offered tempting targets, many Americans believed, for enemy saboteurs.

Hysteria created by the surprise attack on Pearl Harbor produced a flood of rumors that intensified the frenzy. Wild imaginations saw enemy ships and planes where none existed, and panic-stricken citizens concluded with certainty that it was not a question of if, but where and when, secret Japanese agents would suddenly materialize and attack.

Rattled people believed that if the Japanese could attack by surprise in Hawaii, they could attack by surprise again. "A fifth column [a group of fighters working from within a nation in support of military forces—the other four columns—attacking from outside] and espionage network, patiently organized over many years, paved the way for Japan's surprise blow at Pearl Harbor," wrote a reporter for the *New York Times* in the article "Japanese Spies Showed the Way for Raid on Vital Areas in Hawaii," published on December 31, 1941. The reporter explained that U.S. military officers in Hawaii told him that large arrows pointing to military objectives had been meticulously cut in sugar-cane plantation fields situated near the installations; that Japanese vegetable dealers studied U.S. Navy vessels when they delivered supplies and later submitted reports about ship movements, which ships were in port, and where they were berthed; that Japanese aviators shot down in the attack against Pearl Harbor wore school rings from Honolulu high schools and Oregon State University (other newspapers added Stanford University, the University of California, Los Angeles [UCLA] and the University of Southern California [USC] to that list); that Japanese truck drivers weaved from side to side on roads to impede U.S. officers trying to hasten to their posts at Pearl Harbor; and that newspaper ads in Hawaii contained coded messages. He added that 155,000 people of Japanese descent lived in Hawaii, many of whom had "infiltrated" police departments, road construction crews, electric and gas company management, and the telephone service, all "ideal posts for spies." Employing words that could only heighten fears along the West Coast, the reporter concluded, "The facts, if presented to the American people now, may help put them on the alert in other potential areas of danger."[16]

Readers relayed a gripping yarn about an American sailor stationed at Pearl Harbor who had a Japanese wife. According to the tale, which was later proven to be a myth, when the sailor was set to leave home for his post on December 7, his wife, who supposedly knew of the impending attack, begged him to stay away. The sailor ignored his wife's pleas and was at his post when the attack occurred. He survived, then angrily returned home and shot his wife to death.

While the rumor of arrows cut in cane fields produced hysteria along the West Coast, it caused scornful laughter among Hawaiian residents. They knew that the American base at Pearl Harbor was so vast that any enemy force would have little problem locating it. The arrows would be harder to detect than the ships in port, they retorted.

Rumors spiked talk of enemy action on the mainland as well. On December 10 a government agent in San Francisco reported that twenty thousand Japanese residing in the area were prepared to attack, waiting only for a signal from overseas. Despite the fact that only five thousand Japanese Americans lived near San Francisco, people readily believed the report. One newspaper reporter wrote of talk that the Japanese had already established a secret military base south of the Mexican border from which an armed assault could be launched. Another speculated that Japanese American fishermen planned to lay mines across California port entrances, and Japanese American farmers would lace farm produce with arsenic. Some even accused the Issei of purposely purchasing land along dams, railroads, and power lines so they could either spy on them or more readily sabotage them in case of war.

Other reports in the weeks after the December 7 attack placed the Japanese fleet 150 miles (241km) off the California coast or squadrons of enemy air-

An Expression of Loyalty

After Japan attacked Pearl Harbor in Hawaii on December 7, 1941, Japanese Americans quickly took steps to reassure the nation of their loyalty to the United States. *Rafu Shimpo*, a newspaper for the Japanese American community in Los Angeles, California, published the following editorial only three days after the attack:

> The treacherous infamy of Japan's attack upon the United States has united the minds of all Americans, regardless of race, color, or creed. The American people are determined that victory is the supreme objective. The grim determination of a united people has set in motion a tremendous force that will not stop until the Japanese empire is defeated. . . . We are ready to sacrifice our lives to bring a clear-cut victory to the United States. . . . These are indeed dark days, and we [Japanese Americans] feel somewhat lonely that our efforts are not entirely appreciated by all Americans. Suspicion is frequently aroused because of our similarity in facial characteristics to the enemies. But blood ties mean nothing now. We do not hesitate to repudiate and condemn our ancestral country.

The editorial ended with a stirring proclamation: "Japan began this war and it is now up to the United States to end the war by crushing the Japanese empire and her ruthless, barbaric leaders. We have a just cause, a common cause, to fulfill a mission that freedom shall not perish from this earth. Fellow Americans, give us a chance to do our share to make this world a better place to live in!"

Quoted in Lawson Fusao Inada, ed. *Only What We Could Carry*. Berkeley, CA: Heyday Books, 2000, pp. 12–13.

craft over metropolitan and industrial centers. Edward R. Murrow, a radio commentator who gained fame with his broadcasts from London, England, while under attack from German bombers, cautioned a Seattle audience after Pearl Harbor: "I think it's probable that, if Seattle ever does get bombed, you will be able to look up and see some University of Washington sweaters on the boys doing the bombing!"[17]

Most reports proved to be nothing more than the product of fertile imaginations, made more apprehensive by Japan's amazing success in Hawaii. The FBI busted only one spy ring along the West Coast and uncovered no radio broadcasts from that region to Japan. When informed that enemy agents had been the cause of some downed power lines, the FBI investigated and learned that cattle knocking into poles had caused the disruption. Arrow-shaped fires near Seattle alarmed residents and were attributed to the Japanese, but they had actually been started by a farmer burning brush in his field.

People believed what they wanted to believe. When a suspected onslaught of sabotage failed to materialize, many even concluded that this lack of subversive action was proof of disloyalty. The Japanese Americans, who had to be planning some violent deed, were simply biding their time until summoned to action.

Japanese Attacks

Amidst the widespread rumors occurred a few actual attacks along the West Coast that added to the panic. On December 20, 1941 a Japanese submarine torpedoed an American freighter off California. On February 23, 1942 another Japanese submarine shelled an oil refinery near Santa Barbara, California, and although no one was killed, the incident heightened talk of an enemy invasion of California.

Rumors of a Japanese fleet prowling off the coast and of supposed air raids on Los Angeles and other large cities, though never confirmed, combined with the few actual attacks to unnerve residents. Lieutenant General John L. DeWitt, the army commander of the West Coast Defense Command, admonished a group of San Francisco community leaders: "You people do not seem to realize we are at war. So get this: last night there were planes over this community. They were enemy planes. I mean Japanese planes." DeWitt predicted additional bombings and said that anyone who "couldn't take it" had better "get the hell out now, before it comes. And remember, we're fighting the Japanese, who don't respect the laws of war. They're gangsters and they must be treated as such." He added that "only by the grace of God"[18] had California averted serious losses.

As proof, DeWitt only needed to cite the string of victories by the Japanese in the Pacific. Within days of the attack on Pearl Harbor Japan's military forces seized Guam and the Wake Islands from the United States. By the end of December Japan had sent British, American, and Australian forces reeling in Hong Kong, Singapore, and the Philippines. The Japanese had registered so many triumphs that people in the United States began questioning their nation's ability to fight back and wanted to blame someone for Pearl Harbor and the other defeats.

Investigations of the Pearl Harbor attack heightened fears. Both Secretary of the Navy Frank Knox, who inspected Pearl Harbor after the attack, and the official government inquiry into Pearl Harbor headed by Associate Justice of the Supreme Court Owen J. Roberts concluded that Japanese spies and saboteurs played a crucial part in that assault. People along the West Coast, already uncomfortable with the presence of so many Japanese Americans in their midst and wanting to blame someone for Pearl Harbor, directed their venom at that group. Calls for their evacuation from the West Coast began early and gained support as the war continued.

On December 9 the *Los Angeles Times* called California "a zone of danger" and added that of the thousands of Japanese Americans in California, some were good, but the rest created suspicion and distrust. "What the rest may be we do not know, nor can we take a chance in the light of yesterday's demonstration that treachery and double-dealing are major Japanese weapons."[19]

General DeWitt announced that "a Jap's a Jap. . . . It makes no difference whether he is an American citizen or not.

. . . I don't want any of them. . . . There is no way to determine their loyalty."[20] He called the Japanese "gangsters" and said that while he was not concerned about German or Italian Americans, "the Japs we will be worried about all the time until they are wiped off the face of the map."[21]

The *Los Angeles Times* added fuel by stating, "A viper is nonetheless a viper wherever the egg is hatched—so a Japanese-American, born of Japanese parents, grows up to be a Japanese not

An American fighter plane flies over Wake Island in 1942. Japan seized the island from the United States shortly after its attack on Pearl Harbor. Similar successes by Japan heightened fear in the United States.

an American."[22] After interviewing DeWitt, Walter Lippmann, the nation's most influential columnist, took the debate national by writing, "The Pacific Coast is in imminent danger of a combined attack from within and without." He said the Japanese navy had been reconnoitering off the coast, and that "the Pacific Coast is a combat zone: Some part of it may at any moment be a battlefield. And nobody ought to be on a battlefield who has no good reason for being there. There is plenty of room elsewhere for him to exercise his rights."[23]

Another syndicated columnist, Westbrook Pegler, wrote in February 1942 that even if it violated their rights, the Japanese in California should be under armed guard until the war ended. His cohort, columnist Henry McLemore, was even more blunt: "I am for the immediate removal of every Japanese . . . to a point deep in the interior. I don't mean a nice part of the interior either. Herd

In the aftermath of the Pearl Harbor attack, Japanese Americans faced rising discrimination and a curfew. Shop owners and others used signs and badges to highlight their loyalty to the United States. After all, many of them were U.S. citizens.

'em up, pack 'em off and give 'em the inside room in the badlands. Let 'em be pinched, hurt, hungry and dead up against it." He added, "I hate the Japanese. And that goes for all of them."[24]

Pressure Mounts

Not surprisingly, Japanese Americans became targets. Japanese American farmers watched their profits plummet 50 percent in the month after Pearl Harbor, and insurance companies, worried about what damage might be done by irate Americans, canceled policies on Japanese American businesses and homes. A California barber promoted "free shaves for Japs" but would not be held "responsible for accidents," while a funeral parlor owner advertised, "I'd rather do business with a Jap than with an American."[25]

Restaurants hung signs in windows reading, "This Restaurant Poisons Both Rats and Japs,"[26] and a popular pamphlet bore the title, *Slap the Jap Rat*. In an attempt to avoid angry stares or reactions, other Asian Americans placed signs in their cars or wore buttons proclaiming they were Filipinos or Chinese, and not Japanese.

The turmoil lent support to those who advocated the forcible removal of Japanese Americans from the West Coast. Los Angeles mayor, Fletcher Bowron, said on February 6, "Right here in our own city are those who may spring to action at an appointed time in accordance with a prearranged plan wherein each of our little Japanese friends will know his part in the event of any possible attempted invasion or air raid." He added, "We cannot run the risk of another Pearl Harbor episode in Southern California."[27]

When a curfew of 9:00 P.M. was announced on February 4 for enemy aliens, the order did not satisfy the Ventura County Board of Supervisors, which claimed that emotions ran so high on the West Coast that it was no longer safe "for loyal Japanese to reside in close proximity to the Pacific Ocean." The board urged "all persons of the Japanese race"[28] be moved inland 200 miles (322km).

Conditions were ripe for a drastic step, one that would profoundly impact the lives of Japanese Americans, both then and now.

Chapter Two

The Evacuation

As U.S. military forces in the Pacific suffered setbacks in early 1942, anti-Asian attitudes that had been building over a period of decades in the United States, intensified. The slang words *Nip* and *Jap* were commonly used by the press and in official government documents to refer to the Japanese and Japanese Americans, and magazines depicted Japanese as rats, insects, gorillas, and monkeys. A comically exaggerated image of a bespectacled, bucktoothed Japanese soldier appeared on posters and in Hollywood films. At the same time, even though Germany and Italy were also at war with the United States, their soldiers were not nearly as often cast in such a demeaning fashion.

As historian John W. Dower points out, when society views an entire group of people as animals, it makes it easier for that society to treat members of the group as inferior. While the United States eventually devised an evacuation program for Japanese Americans, no similar step was taken against German Americans or Italian Americans, even though the German American Bund, a group supporting German leader Adolf Hitler, listed twenty thousand people on its membership rolls. Their European appearance and background made acceptance in the United States easier than it was for people from Oriental nations.

The Profit Motive

In the climate of the times, various organizations saw an opportunity to gain from the anti-Asian sentiment. The Native Sons and Daughters of the Golden West, an organization promoting the interests of white farmers, had long wanted to ban Japanese Americans, who competed for farmland and crops sales. Politicians hoping to gain public support, labor groups who could help jobless Americans in the absence of Japanese Americans, the American Legion, the California Farm Bureau Federation, the California Joint Immigration Committee, the Western Growers Protective Association, and the Grower-Shipper Vegetable Association all campaigned for evacuation of Japanese Americans from the West Coast. They claimed the move would benefit the nation militarily by keeping enemy spies away from aircraft factories and naval bases, but the real reason lay elsewhere. As a March 1942 magazine article concluded, groups clamoring for evacuation "are endeavoring, under the cover of war-time flag-waving patriotism, to do what they always wanted to do in peacetime: get rid of the Japanese."[29]

A representative of the Grower-Shipper Vegetable Association said as much: "We're charged with wanting to get rid of the Japs for selfish reasons. We might as well be honest. We do. It's a question of whether the white man lives on the Pacific Coast or the brown men. They came into this valley to work, and they stayed to take over."[30]

Japanese American high school student Mary Matsuda Gruenewald noticed the articles casting Japanese as squinty eyed and bucktoothed, inaccurate depictions based upon common stereotypes, and wondered if that was how her classmates saw her. Like any teenager Gruenewald longed for the acceptance of her peers, "but there was no way I could change my skin color, my eyes, my straight black hair, or my name. Shame and self-loathing framed my sense of myself. Yet, that's the way it was—I looked like the enemy." While born in the United States, she had grown up with both American and Japanese influences—one of her favorite meals was fried chicken and sushi—but she did not know if she was American or Japanese. "I wished I had never been born,"[31] she wrote.

A Handful of Defenders

Amidst the outcry, a few individuals and organizations defended the rights of Japanese Americans. Nationally prominent orator Norman Thomas, long a proponent of equality and fair play, stated that evacuation would be seen around the world as an example of American bigotry and racial arrogance. Along with social reformer John Dewey and top religious leaders, Thomas signed a petition asking President Roosevelt to refrain from issuing an evacuation order, and twenty-eight Protestant and Jewish clergymen signed a letter that appeared in the *San Francisco Chronicle* pledging their aid to Japanese Americans.

Henry Grady, secretary of the Pacific Coast Committee on National Security and Fair Play, wondered why a group that, before the war had often been seen as hardworking, now could not be trusted. "Has the setback given to the Allied Arms by the military machine of Japan made our political leaders in state, county and municipality play the bully and turn against our Japanese citizens as a scapegoat for the remote culprits, in Japan, whom our Japanese-American citizens have repeatedly denounced?"[32]

The chairman of a U.S. congressional committee investigating the possible evacuation of Japanese Americans, Representative John H. Tolan of California, believed before the hearings that the West Coast justifiably feared sabotage and alien spies. After listening to testimony, he changed his opinion. Tolan concluded that the fears were based upon nothing more than bigotry and rumor, and that any evacuation would be judged as unconstitutional.

Executive Order 9066

The defenders of Japanese Americans did little to slow the movement toward general evacuation. The first step, in fact, had occurred the same day as the attack on Pearl Harbor. On December 7 the FBI arrested most male residents of Terminal Island, an island near the port of Los Angeles. The island was home to a community of five hundred Japanese American fishermen and their families as well as Naval Air Base San Pedro, a huge U.S. Navy base. Authorities sealed off the town, cut the telephone wires to homes, and took away a few hundred males. The FBI returned on February 1 to remove the remaining males from what the government considered a sensitive area.

President Roosevelt faced enormous pressure from West Coast politicians and interest groups to remove the Japanese Americans. Secretary of War Henry Stimson agreed with the sentiment and said on February 11, "The continued pressure of a large, unassimilated, tightly knit racial group, bound to an enemy nation by strong ties of race, culture, custom and religion along a frontier vulnerable to attack, constituted a menace which had to be dealt with."[33]

Stimson recommended drastic steps even though some top officers in the military did not agree that they were necessary. Army Chief of Staff George C. Marshall assigned Brigadier General Mark W. Clark to evaluate the situation to determine whether the Japanese Americans posed a threat to military installations. Clark concluded there was no need to evacuate every Japanese American, which would tie up as many as fifteen thousand troops. He instead recommended a smaller evacuation of enemy aliens living close to strategic installations. Clark's report did little to counter the call for evacuation.

Swamped with pleas for evacuation, and assured by advisers of its military necessity, Roosevelt issued Executive Order 9066 on February 19, authorizing the War Department to designate certain land as military areas and handing it the right to evacuate from those areas anyone it deemed a threat. Although the order technically applied to the entire nation and to aliens from any nation, Secretary Stimson used it only along the West Coast and only against Japanese Americans, justifying the action on the basis of military need.

"In a drastic move," wrote reporter Lewis Wood in the *New York Times*, President Roosevelt authorized the secretary of war to remove "any or all citizens or aliens from designated military control areas." Attorney General Francis Biddle

Newspapers in California announce the evacuation of Japanese Americans from designated military areas. The evacuation was mobilized after President Franklin D. Roosevelt issued Executive Order 9066.

said that as the affair was a military matter, he doubted any court would investigate it as a violation of civil rights. "The order followed a mounting flood of protests from the West Coast," added Wood, and according to Biddle, "the move has been taken largely for the protection of the Japanese themselves."[34]

On Vashon Island Gruenewald realized the order meant she and her family would have to leave their home and friends for an unknown destination, for an indeterminate number of years. She later wrote that Roosevelt's order was the "decision that took away my world and the life that I had known and loved."[35]

Cooperation

The Japanese American Citizens League (JACL) adopted a friendly attitude with the U.S. government during World War II, hoping that cooperation would result in a lack of bloodshed and more favorable treatment for Japanese Americans. Shortly after Japan attacked the United States in December 1941, the JACL of Seattle, Washington, passed the following resolution of cooperation:

> Whereas the evacuation is a matter of strategic necessity to the safety and defense of the United States;
>
> And, whereas no sacrifice is too great in realizing our avowed objectives in prosecuting this war to a successful conclusion;
>
> And, whereas it is the first duty of loyal Americans to obey their government;
>
> Therefore, be it resolved that the Japanese American Citizens League of Seattle go on record as endorsing cheerful and willing cooperation by the community with the government agencies in carrying out of the evacuation proceedings.

Quoted in *New York Times*. "Pledge Evacuation Aid," April 20, 1942.

Ironically, this order did not affect Japanese Americans residing in Hawaii, the scene of the December 7 attack. That community formed such a large portion of Hawaiian society and business that authorities believed it would be impossible to remove every Japanese American without creating havoc for the rest of Hawaii. Japanese Americans in Hawaii were too valuable to the Hawaiian economy to be so suddenly eliminated. Many even served in important military installations. Authorities maintained a close scrutiny of some individuals but opted not to embark on a mass evacuation similar to what occurred on the mainland's West Coast.

Evacuations Begin

On March 2 General DeWitt issued the first of more than one hundred proclamations. This initial edict divided Washington, Oregon, and California into two portions, Area 1 running along the coast and Area 2 slicing roughly through the middle of the three states. Anyone suspected of espionage, German and Italian American aliens (those who were not citizens), and all persons of Japanese descent, whether alien or citizen, would be excluded from Area 1.

DeWitt urged people to voluntarily move from Area 1 into Area 2, where they would supposedly be able to remain, but fearing the reaction of residents already living in those areas, and trusting that the U.S. government would treat them fairly, fewer than five thousand left their homes. Most decided to let the government handle the issue, and many claimed that they preferred living in locations the government selected, where they could reside under its protection, to traveling alone to an unfamiliar location where they would face the reaction of residents on their own.

A subsequent proclamation by DeWitt widened the exclusion zones to include all of California, Oregon, and Washington, and the western half of Arizona. Some Japanese Americans who had left the first zone now faced the prospect of again gathering their belongings and seeking new quarters elsewhere.

Unless they departed for distant regions, such as the Midwest, those who

Japanese immigrants and their families were urged to voluntarily relocate, but most feared to go somewhere new. Many cities and states, such as Arizona, warned against possible newcomers. Billboards such as this one, preserved today at the Manzanar relocation camp, urged Japanese Americans to stay away.

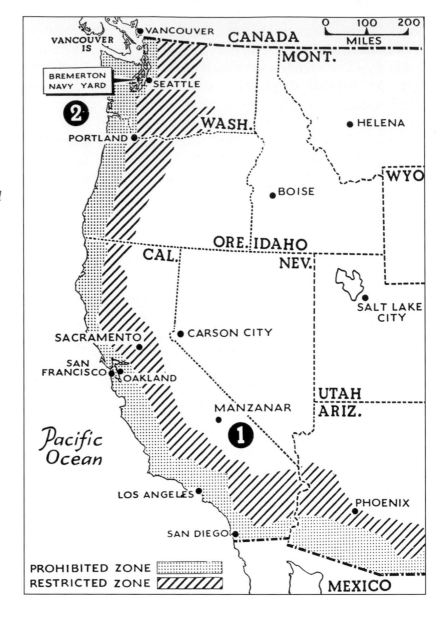

The California coast was declared an exclusion zone where Japanese Americans could not live. In 1942 they were forced to move inland and settle in relocation camps like Manzanar and Bremerton Navy Yard.

PROHIBITED ZONE
RESTRICTED ZONE

left faced immediate hostility. Eastern Californians objected to the presence of people that Western Californians did not want. Patrolmen prevented some Japanese Americans from crossing the border into Kansas, groups of citizens waited at the Nevada border to block evacuees from entering that state, and restaurants and other businesses posted signs requesting that Japanese Americans stay away.

Arizona's governor warned that "we do not propose to be made a dumping ground for enemy aliens from any other State," while Governor Chase Clark of Idaho was even more blunt: "The Japs live like rats, breed like rats and act like rats. We don't want them buying or leasing land or becoming permanently located in our state."[36] Sheriff John Loustalot of Kern County, California, expounded the feelings of thousands of fellow citizens when he announced, "We don't want them here. We don't want any Japs in this county and we wish the government would move them away inland, far from any place where they could do any damage to the national defense effort."[37]

Only one political leader, Governor Ralph Carr of Colorado, welcomed Japanese Americans to his state. He claimed that to preclude their ability to live where they wanted, not just in Colorado but in any state, would violate the Bill of Rights to the U.S. Constitution and would be a blatant attack on long-standing American principles. Governor Carr received bitter criticism from residents in his state and paid for his stand by being voted out of office in the next election.

To prepare for a general evacuation of Japanese Americans from the West Coast, DeWitt had formed the Wartime Civil Control Administration (WCCA) on March 15 with Lieutenant Colonel Karl Bendetsen as its chief administrator. Three days later Roosevelt formed the War Relocation Authority (WRA) with Milton Eisenhower in charge. While the WRA sought locations for permanent camps, the WCCA oversaw the running of temporary assembly centers to which Japanese Americans would first be sent for processing.

Profiteers

While preparations were being made to set up the camps, Japanese Americans faced other problems that were, in some ways, worse than what they later encountered.

To ensure a plentiful harvest General DeWitt asked Japanese American farmers to continue working their fields, even though they would soon have to leave their homes and farms. He explained that by doing so, Japanese Americans would prove their loyalty to their fellow Americans, but as an added measure, he threatened punishment for anyone suspected of sabotaging their crops. Most people cooperated, only to see the results of their labor disappear when they were evacuated from the land shortly before harvesting and deprived of making a profit from their crops. Instead, other individuals moved in, harvested the crops, and pocketed the money, even though the Japanese American tenants had spent their own money nurturing the crops. As a result, some Japanese Americans lost their land and homes because, without the profit from their harvest, they could no longer afford to make mortgage payments.

A few fortunate families were able to place their belongings in storage until after the war or received aid from friendly churches or neighbors who offered basement and attic space for storage. Most, however, did not enjoy such a luxury. Many attempted to sell their businesses, furniture, and personal belongings before they were taken away but had to accept low offers from purchasers who waited until shortly before the evacuation, when frantic owners would be willing to take almost anything in order to avoid gaining nothing. Henry Takemori owned an Arizona grocery store worth $15,000 but accepted $800 from a buyer who made an offer two days before Takemori had to depart, and a druggist sold his $2,000 stock of medicine for $250. Left with little time to dispose of valuables, Japanese Americans "went out to get the best possible prices they could for their goods on short notice,"[38] according to the *New York Times*.

Knowing that families would have to leave soon and that the government would not allow evacuees to take more than a suitcase or two per person, junk men gathered around enclaves of Japanese American homes and businesses to make lowball offers for home furnishings and other belongings. Fred Fujikawa watched a sad scene at Terminal Island, California. Families hurried to collect their possessions, "and here come these junk dealers, these opportunists. This was in December, so a lot of the families had already bought their Christmas presents, like new phonographs or radios, refrigerators. . . . These guys would come in and offer ten or fifteen dollars and because they had to leave, they'd sell."[39]

Jeanne Wakatsuki Houston watched her mother try to sell her beautiful china, but she only received an offer of $15. The set was worth much more and even more in sentiment. She glared at the junk man and took a plate and smashed it on the floor at the dealer's feet. Then, one

by one, she smashed each plate, never once taking her eyes off the dealer. Even after the dealer left in frustration, Houston's mother continued to smash cups and bowls until the entire set was in pieces on the floor.

Cooperation

Despite the hardships, most Japanese Americans cooperated with the government. Leaders of the Japanese American Citizens League (JACL) recommended a peaceful response. The organization's president, Saburo Kido, said cooperation would help win the war. When he and the JACL received criticism for advocating what some saw as a weak response to injustice, he responded that the government would remove Japanese Americans whether they went peacefully or by force, so what choice did they really have? If the JACL urged resistance, bloodshed might occur, and the government would certainly arrest every Japanese American leader, thereby leaving the Japanese American community without guidance. Instead, cooperation would prove their loyalty to the rest of the country.

The editors of the *San Francisco News* typified the feelings that prevailed throughout the nation when they wrote in early March 1942 that while the evacuations would certainly be inconvenient to Japanese Americans, "they must certainly recognize the necessity of clearing the coastal combat areas of all possible fifth columnists and saboteurs. Inasmuch as the presence of enemy agents cannot be detected readily when these

Not the Germans or Italians

As the U.S. government instituted laws that severely restricted the movement of Japanese Americans during World War II, it took few such steps to monitor the movements or abolish the rights of German or Italian Americans. The government quickly eliminated curfews for those groups, failed to issue a general evacuation order, and did not classify noncitizen Italian Americans as aliens, as they did with Japanese Americans. The lenient treatment toward German Americans occurred despite the presence of an active and strong group called the German American Bund, Americans of German descent who supported German leader Adolf Hitler's policies and who had in February 1939 organized a mass rally of twenty thousand Nazi sympathizers at New York City's Madison Square Garden.

This is the Enemy

WINNER R. HOE & CO., INC. AWARD – NATIONAL WAR POSTER COMPETITION
HELD UNDER AUSPICES OF ARTISTS FOR VICTORY, INC. – COUNCIL FOR DEMOCRACY – MUSEUM OF MODERN ART

An anti-Nazi propaganda poster promotes Germans as the enemy. Despite Germany's role in the war, German Americans did not experience as much discrimination or upheaval as Japanese Americans.

areas are thronged by Japanese the only course left is to remove all persons of that race for the duration of the war." The editors stated that evacuations "should be supported by all citizens of whatever racial background, but especially it presents an opportunity to the people of an enemy race to prove their spirit of co-operation and keep their relations with the rest of the population of this country on the firm ground of friendship." According to the editors, the government adopted such a drastic measure to benefit Japanese Americans, for if the government failed to take this step, "real danger would exist for all Japanese if they remained in the combat area. The least act of sabotage might provoke angry reprisals that easily could balloon into bloody race riots."[40]

Eddie Sakamoto, who was married and had three children when he received the order to evacuate, assented peacefully because he thought it was the right thing to do when one's country is at war. He said, "I thought I have to do whatever the government said. This is the war, and we can't do anything, you know. We just have to follow the government order."[41]

Others, like George Ishida of San Francisco, pointed to the violence that could occur if Japanese Americans failed to cooperate and referred to the faith that he and others had in the U.S. government. "Because of racial prejudice against the Japanese, their presence on the Pacific Coast is a cause of disunity among the populace of the Coast," he wrote in a letter to the editor of the *San Francisco News* on April 13, 1942. "In the event of an attempted invasion, it is without a doubt that mob violence would be unleashed against the entire Japanese population. If the Army had to contend with this internal strife as well as the enemy invasion, it would not be able to fully defend our country." He added, "As their small contribution to the war effort, the Japanese will gladly leave their homes, businesses and careers, and, having the utmost faith in America, will place their lives in the hands of the United States Government."[42]

Other Edicts

Later in March General DeWitt announced additional measures. A March 24 proclamation placed a nighttime curfew on Japanese Americans, restricting them to their homes from 8:00 P.M. until 6:00 A.M. The rule also confined Japanese Americans during the day to wherever they worked or to within a radius of 5 miles (8km) around their homes. As many stores, hospitals, and other establishments rested beyond that 5-mile (8km) zone, many Japanese Americans faced serious hardships.

On the same day DeWitt issued the Civilian Exclusion Order Number 1, announcing that fifty Japanese American families living on Bainbridge Island, Washington, had twenty-four hours to gather their belongings for an evacuation to an assembly center the next day. Over the coming weeks, another 107 such evacuations would empty the West Coast of Japanese Americans.

On March 27 DeWitt announced a ban, effective March 29, on voluntary movement from the West Coast to inland regions, thereby trapping every Japanese American who remained in Areas 1 and 2. Although some hastened to leave before the deadline, most had no choice but to stay and face whatever actions the government imposed upon them.

"Hundreds of Bay Area Japanese, convinced at last that the Army is going to carry out its coastal evacuation order, today were leaving for the interior," reported the *San Francisco News* before the deadline. "There was a rush of packing personal belongings and disposing of property that could not be carried in autos or trucks, as the deadline for departure neared. After Sunday night no Japanese—alien or citizen—may leave the military area voluntarily."[43]

In late March army units arrived to begin the movement to assembly centers. Notices posted on telephone poles and in store windows announced that the head of each Japanese family should report to the local civil control station to pick up tags bearing the family's number that

Two U.S. Army medics escort a Japanese woman to a ferry at Bainbridge Island, Washington, which she has been forced to evacuate. Japanese American families on the island had twenty-four hours to pack and leave their homes.

What to Take

When teenager Mary Matsuda Gruenewald and her family received the U.S. government's order to evacuate their Vashon Island, Washington, home, they faced the problem of what to pack in their two suitcases per person and what items to leave behind. In her book, *Looking Like the Enemy*, Gruenewald explains that her family discussed the situation and decided that each of them would take:

- one pair of sheets
- a pillowcase
- one blanket
- one heavy winter overcoat
- several sweaters
- two blouses or shirts
- two slacks or skirts
- a week's worth of socks and underwear
- one pair of shoes
- a flannel nightgown or pajamas
- personal toilet articles
- silverware, a cup, a plate

Mary Matsuda Gruenewald. *Looking Like the Enemy*. Troutdale, OR: NewSage Press, 2005, p. 31.

were to be affixed to each piece of luggage and carried by each family member. They were told to bring bedding and linen for each person, toilet articles, knives, forks, spoons, bowls, and whatever clothing and personal effects that could fit into two suitcases per person. They learned to their dismay that family pets had to be left behind. Some observers remarked that the posters and information bore a chilling resemblance to soldiers posting restrictions of Jewish rights in Nazi Germany.

Leaving Home

"The greatest forced migration in American history was getting under way today,"[44] wrote the *San Francisco News* on March 4, 1942, as more than one hundred thousand Japanese Americans living along the West Coast prepared to leave their family homes for the uncertain world of detention camps. Some of the younger evacuees considered it an adventure of sorts, but the older Japanese Americans took a more somber approach. They had no idea how long they would be held, what the conditions would be like, or what awaited them back home once they returned, if ever. Parents worried about their children, whose tender lives were being disrupted, and whether they could create any sort of "normal" world for boys and girls who should be scampering around playgrounds, working on homework, or making their first awkward attempt to ask someone to a dance.

Mary Tsukamoto was concerned about her grandparents, who had lived on the same land for fifty years but now had to leave all that was familiar. "It was a cruel thing to do to them in their twilight years,"[45] she recalled. Tsukamoto was touched that some of her grandparents' neighbors offered to keep some items, such as the piano and the family dining table, until after the war but witnessed her grandparents quietly watch as opportunists grabbed up possessions accumulated over a lifetime they could not take with them to camp.

Tsukamoto, who felt safe in the Japanese American community in her hometown, was crushed when she learned that authorities divided her hometown into sectors and that everyone would not be going to the same center. Friends would no longer see each other, and family members who lived in different parts of town went to different centers.

The day of departure proved agoniz-ing for thousands of Japanese Americans throughout the West Coast. The moment when Tsukamoto and others had to say good-bye to their pets and gardens, their rooms and swing sets, was especially traumatic. "I remember that sad morning when we realized suddenly that we wouldn't be free. It was such a clear, beautiful day, and I remember as we were driving, our tears."[46]

Many, like Ben Iijima's family, meticulously cleaned their homes before leaving. They used soap and water to clean the kitchen, repainted the sink, trimmed the hedges outside, washed every window, and weeded their garden. They knew they might not see their home for a long time, but it was all they had, and they wanted to leave it spotless, as if that might somehow help bring them quickly back.

Gruenewald's family destroyed phonograph records, family photographs, exquisite Japanese dolls, and books of classic Japanese literature. As they tossed each photograph into the fire, they tearfully asked forgiveness from the person in the photo. Most painful for Gruenewald was tossing into the flames the beautiful dolls depicting Japanese ladies in waiting at the emperor's court that she had treasured her entire life. She longed to keep them, and many other items she had collected through the years, but how do you cram a lifetime of possessions into two suitcases? What do you keep? What do you leave behind? Can you justify holding onto dolls when an extra outfit of clothes would be more sensible? Some parents told their sons and daughters to wear as many layers of clothing as they could stand so there would be more room in the suitcases for other things.

Gruenewald said that it might not have mattered to the authorities who wrenched them from everything they loved, "but for our family we began to feel the little deaths that would haunt us for years as we faced our fate as Japanese-Americans during World War II." They had committed no crime, but "in the end, all that mattered to the United States government was what we looked like."[47]

Gruenewald's father arranged for a deputy sheriff who lived on Vashon Island to look after the family farm. As they prepared to leave, her mother reminded them of how blessed they had been, and that the good times they experienced at their home would help them endure whatever lay ahead. Gruenewald patted her cat, Kitty, and her dog, Frisky, then turned away in silence. As they left, they "took one final look through our tears at our beloved home." She added, "The unknown was overwhelmingly and terrifyingly unimaginable. So many questions whirled around in my head that I could scarcely focus on any one thought." Would she, for instance, be able to graduate from high school? Her father, she noticed, stared straight ahead rather than glancing toward his family, as if one look would shatter him. "A resolute look on his face belied the realization that he could not protect his family from this looming threat."[48] Could anything be more difficult for a parent, Gruenewald wondered, than facing the inability to safeguard his children and provide the safe, secure world every child deserves?

When the family arrived at the town station, Gruenewald spotted soldiers with rifles and fixed bayonets. She noticed fear in her father's face, the first time she had ever seen him anything but composed, and felt her own courage wane. "Seeing him defeated terrified me,"[49] said Gruenewald of the father in whose strength she had placed such faith.

Gruenewald's family boarded army trucks for the ride through town to the ferry dock. They passed all the familiar sights that had made growing up on Vashon Island idyllic—the Methodist church in which they worshipped, the local theater, the post office with its American flag waving in the breeze, Vashon Grade School, and the gymnasium in which Gruenewald had played with her friends.

They arrived at the dock to see many non-Japanese friends waiting to say good-bye. One classmate told Gruenewald how wrong the evacuation was, and another made her promise to write letters from camp. The local church offered tea and sandwiches, and other neighbors wished them good fortune. Gruenewald noticed, however, that other people were not as friendly, with one man shouting, "Get outta here, you God damned Japs! I oughta blast your heads off."[50]

The Japanese government vehemently protested the forcible removal of people of Japanese descent, labeling it

Japanese Americans line up to board a bus that will take them to an internment camp. They could only take what would fit into two suitcases and were forced to leave pets behind.

"diabolic savagery." A broadcast out of Tokyo claimed that "neutral observers said obviously the constitutional rights of those American-born Japanese have been ruthlessly trampled upon in the heat of resentment aroused by American political and military errors" and added that "the viciousness of the American Government in persecuting a helpless, strictly civilian and manifestly innocent minority will remain in history as one of the blackest crimes ever committed by the so-called great powers."[51]

Few in the United States agreed with Tokyo, however. In a time of fear and uncertainty, Americans wanted reassurance that all was safe and that their government took whatever steps necessary to ensure their security. In the process, the government disrupted the worlds of Mary Matsuda Gruenewald and thousands of Japanese Americans.

Chapter Three

Introduction to Camp Life

By June 1, 1942, authorities had removed almost every Japanese American from Area 1, and by month's end evacuations had been completed in 109 zones in Areas 1 and 2. More than one hundred thousand individuals, ranging from newborn infants to aging grandparents, entered first an assembly center and then a permanent camp.

Assembly Centers

The main responsibility of the Wartime Civil Control Administration (WCCA) was to erect and administer eighteen temporary assembly centers, including fourteen in California, that would house the evacuees until ten permanent relocation centers were constructed. Japanese Americans lived in these assembly centers roughly from March 1942 to October 1942.

Most Japanese Americans never forgot when they first saw their tempo-

rary homes. One person said in a letter to a friend that he did not consider the evacuation unfair until he saw the rifle-wielding soldiers, the machine guns, the 20-foot-high (6.1m) guard towers, and the searchlights. Mary Matsuda Gruenewald wondered why, if the centers had been established for their safety, the barbed wire pointed inward at them instead of outward toward the outside world. Mary Tsukamoto took one look at the residents who were already in camp and was reminded of animals in a zoo, staring out from behind their cages.

Authorities processed each new group as it arrived. They inspected all belongings to remove any items they considered threatening, conducted brief medical examinations, filled out background forms for each person, and assigned living quarters.

Most assembly centers were tar-paper covered wooden barracks divided into compartments, offering 20 by 24 feet (6.1m by 7.3m) of living space. Each living space contained army cots, blankets, and a bare lightbulb hanging from the center of the ceiling. At many centers men were given large sacks and told to go to the back of camp, where they were to fill the bags with straw to use as mattresses. Partitions divided the compartments, but since they did not go all the way to the ceiling, noise from any compartment—a crying baby, laughter, arguments, loud snoring—could be heard everywhere. Fourteen barracks composed a block of about eight hundred people, each with its own mess hall, laundry, and recreation center.

Some camps were set up in former fairgrounds or in racetracks, where families lived in horse stalls. At Santa Anita Park, a racetrack in Arcadia, California,

Evacuated Japanese arrive at Puyallup, Washington's assembly center, a temporary residence before they could be sent on to a permanent relocation center. The assembly centers were made of wood, and beds had straw mattresses. Conditions were crowded, with no running water and little privacy.

the horses had been removed only four days before the first group of evacuees arrived. Even though the stalls had been whitewashed, straw and horsehair clung to the fresh paint, and the stalls reeked of manure. Matters worsened in the summer heat, when the smell attracted large horse flies and forced people to remain outside the stalls.

Inconvenience ruled. Because compartments did not have running water, people had to walk to common taps to obtain whatever water the family needed. People became accustomed to waiting in line to eat and to use the latrine or the showers. Latrines were little more than raised wooden platforms with holes cut out. Even though partitions separated the holes, a lack of doors prevented any privacy.

For some, the verbal taunts overshadowed any physical discomfort. "What really hurts most," wrote Ted Nakashima, "is the constant reference to us evacuees as 'Japs.' 'Japs' are the guys we are fighting. We're on this side, and we want to help."[52]

Into the Camps

The government transferred evacuees from the assembly centers to the permanent camps as soon as they were ready. Families often had little warning of an impending move. A train pulled in, and the next day soldiers led them to the waiting rail cars for transportation to an unknown location. Rumors of a desert locale or some other forlorn spot had parents guessing as to what would become of their families.

The trips in the uncomfortable train cars, which started near the end of May 1942, lasted several days. As sleeping quarters were provided only for infants and those with physical handicaps, most people had to sit the entire way, eating and sleeping in their seats. Poor ventilation forced everyone to travel in stifling conditions, and the slow-moving trains often had to pull to the sidings to allow faster-moving troop and equipment trains to speed by.

The trip was a "nightmare," according to Mine Okubo, who went to Topaz in Utah. The outdated train "was covered with dust, and as the gaslights failed to function properly we traveled in complete darkness most of the night."[53] Soldiers kept the shades drawn over the windows around the clock and forbade the evacuees from looking outside. People, either due to motion sickness or fear, became ill and vomited, and children cried as the train traveled across the countryside. One time Okubo's train stopped to permit the evacuees to stretch their legs for half an hour, but Okubo noticed even that movement was restricted—on both sides of the tracks barbed-wire fences bordered the area in which they strolled, and a soldier stood every 15 feet (4.6m).

Their worries increased when they arrived at one of the ten camps that would be their new home for an indeterminate amount of time. Government workers had reassured them that their living quarters would be more comfortable and would offer more freedom than the assembly centers, but an initial

On arrival at one of the ten internment camps, evacuees were met with the scary sight of barbed wire and guard towers, like the one here from Manzanar. Families used to the comforts of home now had to live in the confined space of barracks, with little privacy and a lot of rules.

examination countered those assurances. Eight-foot-high (2.4m) barbed-wire fences surrounded the area, and armed guards manned watchtowers at each corner. Searchlights swept the camp, and machine guns belied the thought of more freedom. "I just cried," said Haruko Niwa when he first saw Manzanar. "I thought, well, we just have to accept this situation and do the best we can."[54]

Joyous welcomes lent an air of unreality for people about to be placed behind fences. A Boy Scout band, playing "Hail,

Hail, the Gang's All Here," greeted people at Topaz, while Japanese Americans who were already camp residents held a banner saying, "Welcome to Topaz, the Jewel of the Desert." Evacuees did not know whether to cry or laugh scornfully at the strange sight.

People were directed first to the mess halls for processing, which took a few hours. Interviewers sitting at long tables asked questions about former occupations to help determine which jobs the evacuees might be qualified for in camp,

Propaganda Uses

Even though most Americans favored the internment of Japanese Americans after the Japanese attack on Pearl Harbor, some voices of protest appeared. In 1944, *Fortune* magazine, a publication that normally focuses on business matters, printed an article explaining how the internment handed Japan a convenient propaganda tool. It said that Americans did not

> realize what persistent and effective use Japan has been able to make, throughout the entire Far East, of U.S. imprisonment of persons of Japanese descent. The propaganda concerns itself less with *how* the U.S. treats the people imprisoned than *who* was imprisoned. By pointing out, again and again, that the U.S. put behind fences well over 100,000 people of Japanese blood, the majority of them citizens of the U.S., Japan describes to her Far Eastern radio audiences one more instance of American racial discrimination. To convince all Orientals that the war in the Pacific is a crusade against the white man's racial oppression, the enemy shrewdly notes every occurrence in the U.S. that suggests injustice to racial minorities, from the Negroes to the Mexicans and Japanese.

Fortune. "Issei, Nisei, Kibei," April 1944, p. 8.

fingerprinted each person, administered brief physicals, and then had them swear loyalty to the government. Volunteers handed out copies of the camp newspaper, which contained helpful information about their new home as well as a list of the camp's rules.

When the processing was complete, the evacuees were then shown to their quarters, rows of military-style barracks offering little privacy or space. The first sight of the barracks unnerved many newcomers as they tried to comprehend living in such confined areas that lacked comfortable living rooms and separate bedrooms for each family member. One government worker who processed the evacuees learned to remain outside when the families entered their new quarters. "It was too terrible to witness the pain in people's faces, too shameful for them to be seen in this degrading situation."[55]

The WRA

Once the evacuees arrived at their permanent camp, they came under the jurisdiction of the War Relocation Authority (WRA). The WRA was responsible for providing a decent place for them to live and for arranging activities, work, and daily schedules during their confinement. Its top administrator, Milton Eisenhower, at first thought he could help resettle the evacuees elsewhere throughout the nation and create a number of Japanese American communities in other states, but opposition by state governors halted that plan before it got off the ground. One governor even went so far as to caution Eisenhower, "If you bring Japanese into my state, I promise you they will be hanging from every tree."[56]

Faced with such strong opposition, Eisenhower knew he would have to hold Japanese Americans in camps until war emotions calmed. He planned to establish work camps similar to those of Roosevelt's during the Great Depression in the 1930s that had created jobs for out-of-work citizens. Eisenhower believed that Japanese Americans could utilize their time in camp to create products helpful to the war effort, make money, and gain the admiration of their fellow Americans. He recognized, though, that confining American citizens of any national origin violated everything for which the country stood. He wrote to a friend, saying, "When the war is over and we consider calmly this unprecedented migration of 120,000 people, we as Americans are going to regret the unavoidable injustices that may have been done."[57]

Military motives could no longer be used to justify the camps, as the fortunes of war in the Pacific had begun to favor the United States. Although a long road that included bitter fighting and many deaths still lay ahead, the U.S. Navy had turned aside the Japanese fleet in a monumental June 1942 clash off Midway Island in the central Pacific. By sinking four crucial Japanese aircraft carriers, American naval forces halted the eastward movement of the Japanese navy and ended the threat to the West Coast that so alarmed area citizens and politicians. If, as many contended, Japanese Americans had to be evacuated because of a military threat, they should now be allowed to return to their homes because that reason no longer existed. The opposite occurred. By the time of the Midway battle, only seventeen thousand had been evacuated, but instead of halting the process, another ninety-three thousand went to the camps.

The WRA eventually established camps, officially called relocation centers, at ten locations in seven states—Manzanar and Tule Lake in California, Poston and Gila River on Indian reservations in Arizona, Topaz in central Utah, Amache (also called Granada) in Colorado, Heart Mountain in Wyoming, Minidoka in Idaho, and Rohwer and Jerome in Arkansas. By November 1, 1942, trains had transported 110,000 persons of Japanese descent into the camps.

The army placed restrictions on where the camps could be located. It insisted that they be established in isolated places away from important military installations, such as military camps and aircraft factories, but close enough to railroads and major highways for easy transportation. The WRA concluded that the camps had to have adequate water, adequate sources of power, and at least

7,500 acres (3,035ha) of land for farming. The camps also had to be on land owned or controlled by the government and located some distance from towns and cities. Everyone agreed that under no circumstance could any whites be displaced because of a camp. These restrictions severely limited the options, forcing the WRA to settle on places where no one else wanted to live, such as snake-infested swamps (Rohwer and Jerome in Arkansas) and deserts (seven camps). Only Tule Lake, situated on a dry lake bed, offered ground suitable for farming.

Almost overnight the centers bloomed into towns of their own. By June 1942 Manzanar had seven hundred one-story-buildings standing on 600 acres (243ha) of land, including barracks, mess halls, recreation halls, laundries, and separate men's and women's lavatories and showers. The other camps followed suit, quickly erected makeshift barracks and mess halls to service their ever-expanding communities.

Helpers and Critics

Eisenhower and his WRA workers found themselves in a difficult situation. They had to administer a system that many concluded had unjustly confined thousands, but they wanted do so in a way that reduced the hardships for those incarcerated. If they offered too many amenities to the Japanese Americans, however, they received biting criticism from politicians, newspapers, and citizens who thought the Japanese Americans should be confined with only

the basic necessities. If they provided too little, innocent people, including babies and the elderly, suffered.

E.R. Fryer, a field director for the WRA, explained in a 1942 *New York Times* article why so many of his workers took extraordinary measures to assist Japanese Americans, saying that the camps offered a chance for his workers to act according to the principles for which the nation's military then fought Germany and Japan: "Just because these people are Japanese, there is no reason why they should not be treated decently and humanely by white Americans, who have a heavy obligation to be tolerant." He added, "Our job is to mitigate the tragic consequences of the program, to prevent these people from becoming human wreckage and at the same time to make it possible for Japanese Americans to contribute greatly to the war effort."[58] The efforts of the WRA helped stop a tragic situation from spiraling into a worse nightmare for Japanese Americans.

Some individuals and organizations criticized the evacuation, although their arguments foundered against an overwhelming sentiment that favored the program. A group called the Tolan Committee claimed the incarceration of so many Japanese Americans would be a flagrant waste of government money and would mean deportation to Japan after the war for everyone detained. How, the committee wondered, could anyone expect Japanese Americans to be loyal to a government that had so harshly taken away their livelihoods and homes?

The *Christian Century*, a religious publication, wrote in June 1942 that the policy violated the constitutional rights of every Japanese American and officially made racial discrimination a part of governmental policy. "It [the U.S. government] is moving in the same direction Germany moved,"[59] the paper warned.

Joe Kurihara, a Hawaiian-born Nisei and a veteran of World War I, expressed the outrage military veterans of other wars felt at being shunned by a country that had asked for their service a quarter of a century earlier. "I was wounded fighting for the United States. I draw compensation for my wounds from the United States government while rotting in a United States concentration camp. These are the scars I have, keepsakes of my Army service for this country. It is no longer my country. I am now a hundred percent Japanese. I spit on these scars of the United States."[60]

A WRA assistant project director who heard Kurihara express his feelings did not blame the veteran. The administrator claimed that he would be bitter, too, if this had happened to him.

Housing

Since every camp except Manzanar, which had been constructed as an assembly center and thus already possessed many of the structures required to house the flood of people, was built simultaneously, each featured the same basic design. The trademark feature that made the greatest impact upon residents was the barbed-wire fences connecting watchtowers containing armed guards that surrounded the barracks and administrative offices.

Most camps were incomplete when the first evacuees arrived. Little was actually set up when Jeanne Wakatsuki Houston arrived at Manzanar. She wrote that it was "pure chaos. That's the only way to describe it. The evacuation had been so hurriedly planned, the camps so hastily thrown together, nothing was completed when we got there, and almost nothing worked."[61] With wartime shortages making construction materials hard to obtain, the WRA turned to makeshift remedies and erected barracks fashioned from plywood and tar paper.

The camps featured "blocks" of twelve to fourteen barracks in which the internees resided. Each block contained a mess hall that could feed the nearly three hundred people inhabiting the block, common toilet and shower facilities for males and females, a laundry, and a recreation hall.

Internees, accustomed to living in their own homes, now had to make do in barracks with four to six other families, almost always strangers. Standing 20 feet (6.1m) tall, 100 feet (30m) wide, and 120 feet (37m) long, the barracks were divided into sections, one or two for each family depending upon the number in the family.

The living quarters offered little more than a place to sleep. "Not only did we stop eating at home," wrote Houston of her stay at Manzanar, "there was no longer a home to eat in. The cubicles we had were too small for anything you might call 'living.'"[62] Each family had what the government called an apartment, which was merely a section of their barracks containing wooden partitions that stopped short of the ceiling and were so thin that, as happened in the assembly centers, one could hear every noise in the entire barracks.

Averaging 16 feet by 19 feet (4.9m by 5.8m) in dimensions, the apartments offered little privacy and minimal room to live as a family unit. They lacked running water—people had to walk to the common water center with buckets to obtain their daily supply—and had almost no furniture. There were canvas cots for sleeping, coal stoves for heating, and a solitary lightbulb hanging from the ceiling.

George Takei, who later starred as Mr. Sulu in the *Star Trek* television series and movies, recalled that his parents jammed five beds into one of the two rooms the family had at Tule Lake so they could free the other to use during the day. Only five years old but the oldest of the family's three children, Takei slept at the end, farthest from his parents so his two younger siblings could be nearer their mother.

A family sits in their living quarters at the Manzanar camp. Barracks were partitioned to provide privacy, but the thin partitions did not block noise. Families decorated their quarters as best they could with limited resources.

Husbands and fathers eventually added minor improvements, foraging around camp for pieces of scrap wood or metal to fashion rudimentary furniture and partitions. Paint and curtains of cloth made interiors a bit more enticing, and vegetable gardens eventually beautified the area and provided an extra source of nourishment. Empty suitcases made passable tables, and pieces of tin covered knotholes in the walls or cracks in the floors.

Toilet and shower facilities made daily life even more difficult. For the first year at Minidoka, residents had to use outhouses since the proper sewer systems and facilities had not yet been built. Elsewhere, twelve toilet bowls arranged in six pairs, back-to-back and lacking partitions, served as toilet facilities, while a long metal trough with hot and cold spigots stretched along one wall. "My mother was a very modest person," wrote Houston of her mother's discomfort at having to use a common toilet facility, "and this was going to be agony for her, sitting down in public, among strangers."[63] Her mother gradually adjusted, telling her family it was something over which she lacked control and thus must accept it.

To take a shower or use the toilet facilities, people often had to walk a mile (1.6km) or more, meaning that in the summer heat, residents became drenched in sweat on their way home from taking a shower. Many waited until late at night to shower or use the latrine, hoping to find fewer people around. Takei recalled the grueling experience of having to use a latrine so far away: "Sometimes it was sheer torture dashing through the wind, muscles tightly held, to the latrine. There were occasions when I didn't think I could make it in time."[64]

At one end of the camps stood the administrative staff's quarters. Military police and camp personnel lived in larger, better-furnished apartments that included cooling systems, refrigerators, and indoor toilets and baths.

Basic Needs

Three times a day bells rang to signal mealtime, and the barracks in each block emptied as people headed to the mess halls for a filling, if not very exciting, meal. Young and old again had to walk as much as a mile (1.6km) to reach the mess hall, and depending upon the food available and the skill of the cooks preparing it, the meal could be either quite decent or depressingly unappealing.

The WRA wanted to offer better meals, but it was restricted in what it could provide. It could hardly serve steak and a wide selection of desserts when Americans elsewhere were scrambling to put a decent meal on the table and American soldiers fighting oversees were eating cold army rations from a can. The WRA policy stated that internees should receive the same variety of foods as the rest of the nation and that the meals could not cost more than the fifty cents per day the government allocated for military personnel. If food items, such as sugar and certain meats, were rationed on the outside due to wartime shortages, then they would be rationed in the same quantities to the camps.

Hot dogs, fish, rice, and macaroni and cheese composed a large portion of the diet at many camps, and meatless dinners were all too frequent. Camp gardens added lettuce, corn, tomatoes, beans, and other vegetables, while makeshift farms offered chickens and eggs, turkeys, and other products. No one starved—a small percentage of people actually ate a bit better than they previously had—but few raved about their meals in letters to friends on the outside.

When they evacuated, people had carried with them as much clothing as they could, but once in camp, they sometimes found that their clothing failed to meet their needs. Those who had previously lived in warmer climes brought clothes ill suited for harsh snowy winters in mountain camps or in windswept desert areas. The Sears catalog, from which people could order clothing and an enticing array of other items, proved popular to those who had extra money to spend, while mothers' and grandmothers' sewing magic fashioned extra shorts or blouses from fabric and bits of cloth.

Mainly due to shortages of doctors and nurses, medical care often failed to match the outside world and caused delays in treatment. The Jerome camp had only seven physicians to care for ten thousand people in late 1942. Most camps instituted a rushed training program to add nurse's aides, but the volunteers often felt their training fell short of what they needed. One aide at Topaz claimed that she could not even name the various instruments she was expected to handle and said that her inadequate training made her uncomfortable in dealing with people who looked to her for help.

Illnesses often raced through the barracks because so many internees were so closely confined. Epidemics of dysentery briefly flared at some camps, while a typhoid epidemic raged at Minidoka. Doctors had few facilities to tend to those with special needs or those with serious medical ailments, requiring treatment at outside hospitals, and mentally impaired children or children with tuberculosis and other ailments sometimes had to be separated from parents.

Despite the problems, medical care was free, and physicians emphasized preventive medicine through healthy lifestyles. The government also established immunization programs at each camp. A 1946 study found that the incarcerated Japanese Americans experienced a lower death rate than that of the general population outside the camps.

Camp Administration and Security

The WRA's camp administrators did their best to establish as normal a lifestyle as possible in the camps. Each camp had departments overseeing personnel, maintenance, employment, social welfare, medical, farm, and school needs. WRA analysts and psychologists interviewed internees, and WRA staff made recommendations to administrators to assist them in running the camps.

The internment camps provided for basic needs, including food and medical care. Internees receive dental care at an internment camp in 1942.

The WRA allowed community councils and block managers to help them run the camps. Representatives to the community council, the official spokesmen for the Japanese American community, were selected from each block in a camp-wide election. They assisted the chief administrator by making suggestions and by serving as a conduit for communication between camp administration and those interned. Councils could vote on measures, but every item was subject to the administrator's veto. Issei were barred from serving on the councils, as they were not U.S. citizens, which meant the councils were manned only by the younger internees.

Assisting the community councils were block managers, men who governed each block. Generally appointed by the administrator and often an Issei, the block manager made sure that internees had the food, housing, and medical care they required, supervised the maintenance of the block barracks and grounds, and conveyed WRA information and regulations to the block residents. Paid a monthly wage of sixteen dollars, the men gained the respect of both administrators and residents.

Ironically, now that the Japanese Americans were behind fences, some felt a sense of relief and security that they had lacked when they were outside. A *New York Times* reporter observed in June 1942 that for the first time since Pearl Harbor, many residents at Manzanar did not live in fear over what might happen at the hands of angry non-Japanese Americans. They could no longer be blamed for any mysterious incidents, such as flashing lights in the ocean or supposed sabotage, that earlier had gained the indignation of non-Japanese Americans.

They paid a heavy price for that sense of security, however. "Camp wasn't a dreadful place," said Helen Murao of Minidoka. "It wasn't a wretched place, but I think the most significant thing for me was our loss of freedom."[65] No matter how secure, internees needed only to glance at the barbed wire fences and armed guards to know that, for the foreseeable future, they were in a place not of their own choosing, far from home and friends. They could not travel where they wanted or work at a place of their own choosing. They could not go to the theater or to see a major sporting event. Soldiers inspected every package mailed from the outside to make certain it contained nothing illegal or threatening.

Coddling

The War Relocation Authority (WRA), the agency created by President Franklin D. Roosevelt to manage the internment camps, often received criticism for what some considered to be coddling, or pampered treatment, of the Japanese Americans interned in the camps. *Fortune* magazine had an apt response to those who leveled such charges:

> No one who has visited a relocation center and seen the living space, eaten the food, or merely kept his eyes open could honestly apply the word "coddling" to WRA's administration of the camps. The people are jammed together in frame barracks. The only privacy possible is achieved by hanging flimsy cotton curtains between the crowded beds. Furniture is improvised from bits of scrap lumber: a box for a table, three short ends of board made into a backless chair. The family's clothing and few personal possessions are somehow stuffed neatly away—on shelves of scrap lumber, a priceless commodity in all camps, if available. Otherwise, they are stuffed away under the beds.

Fortune. "Issei, Nisei, Kibei," April 1944, p. 74.

The presence of those guards, patrolling the fences twenty-four hours a day, was a constant reminder that the internees were isolated from everything friendly and familiar.

Gruenewald feared that one day those soldiers would turn their rifles on her and kill her. John Tateishi remembers his mother glancing at the guard tower in fear and warning him to stay away from the fence. Some may have felt protected inside the camps, but it came at the cost of losing contact with the outside world and the society they longed to rejoin one day.

At the same time, Japanese Americans made the best of an unfortunate situation. Even in the midst of misery, daily life has a way of rolling on.

Chapter Four

Daily Life in Camp

From June 1943 to August 1943 the popular comic strip *Superman* published episodes in which the hero, disguised as newspaper reporter Clark Kent, and reporter Lois Lane visit every facility available to the Japanese Americans, including the schools, and learn that even though the Japanese Americans had been forcibly removed from their West Coast homes, they experienced a pleasant existence inside the camps. An escort informs Kent and Lane that the government "has done all but lean over backwards in its desire to be humane and fair."[66]

While the WRA did attempt to make life more comfortable for camp residents, few Japanese Americans agreed with the rosy portrayal that appeared in hundreds of newspapers across the nation as the fictional superhero toured an internment facility. Although interned youngsters still shot marbles, played baseball with friends, watched movies, and listened to current songs over the radio, camp reality clashed with the views presented by the *Superman* comic strip.

Nature

Nature offered the internees the first indication that life inside an isolated camp was dramatically different from their former lives. "We were given a rousing welcome by a dust storm," recalled Monica Sone of her first day at Minidoka. "We felt as if we were standing in a gigantic sand-mixing machine as the sixty-mile [-per-hour] gale lifted the loose earth up into the sky, obliterating everything. Sand filled our mouths and nostrils and stung our faces and hands like a thousand darting needles."[67] Sone and her family stumbled to their living quarters, gasping for air as the window panes rattled and dust poured through wall cracks.

Mary Matsuda Gruenewald found the same at Tule Lake, where desert storms suddenly appeared and lashed the camp for ten to fifteen minutes "like a thousand bees were stinging our hands and faces."[68] Residents could taste the dirt and grit in their mouths and feel it scratching under their clothes.

At the storms' heights people at Topaz could barely see 3 feet (0.9m) ahead, and afterward they walked in a layer of fine dust an inch (2.5cm) thick. Dust filtered underneath bed covers and blanketed buildings and furniture.

People suffered through sweltering summer days in desert camps, where temperatures soared over 100°F (38°C), then plunged below freezing during cold winter months. The two Arkansas camps experienced humid summers with clouds of mosquitoes that infested every barracks.

During the summers, internees often dug cellars 6 feet (1.8m) deep to avoid the heat and dust. In winter many people found that the clothing they had

In 1943 the popular comic strip character Superman visited an internment camp and announced they were comfortable camps. This fictional account presented a positive image of the camps, where so many were forced to relocate.

brought from home was inadequate to fend off the bitter cold and had to turn to surplus army coats and jackets handed out by administrators.

Snakes and other animals made life uneasy as well. Desert rattlesnakes and scorpions were common sights, as were black widow spiders, centipedes, mosquitoes, and poisonous Gila monsters. The two Arkansas camps, which were located in swamps, were infested by four of the deadliest snakes in the United States.

Daily Schedules

Every day began with a siren sounding at 7:00 A.M., rousing everyone for a cafeteria-style breakfast served in the mess hall. Work for those adults who volunteered for maintenance, police, or one of the other many jobs offered in camp, commenced at 8:00 A.M., while students arrived at schools for an 8:30 or 9:00 A.M. start. Housewives tended to the laundry and cared for the apartment, while those with free time had the option of attending one of the various educational and crafts classes offered in camp. Lunch from 11:30 A.M. to 12:30 P.M. and dinner from 5:00 to 6:00 P.M. gave people the chance to share their days and mingle with friends, while the evenings were free to visit, listen to the radio, play baseball, attend a movie, or participate in other activities.

Racing from one spot to the next became a distinguishing feature of camp life. The children scampered to mess halls to grab their meals with friends, while everyone learned that if they

hoped to launder their clothes or take a shower with hot water, they had best rush to those facilities before the supply ran out.

To avoid establishing a system in which large numbers of people depended totally upon the government for their living, the WRA provided employment opportunities in camp. Although not matching the outside world in pay scale, the jobs, available to any internee aged sixteen or older, at least gave the workers a chance to feel as if they were contributing to their family's welfare. Putting most individuals to work also reduced the amount of idle time, which might strengthen hostile feelings about the incarceration as people focused on their miseries.

The WRA instituted a pay scale for the internees, but when newspapers reported that Japanese Americans were to be paid more than soldiers fighting overseas, a flood of protests forced the WRA to backpedal. It assured critics that the internees would not receive benefits greater than the military salary of seventy dollars per month, and it set limits of twelve dollars per month for unskilled workers, such as gardeners and typists; sixteen dollars per month for bakers, barbers, and other skilled trades; and nineteen dollars per month for professional and technical workers, such as teachers, doctors, and accountants.

Japanese Americans had no choice but to accept the relatively low pay, which they saw as yet another injustice in a world of unfairness. Most of them had already suffered great financial

A number of jobs were available at the relocation camps, from maintenance and police to bakers, teachers, reporters, and nurses. Despite all of the work that they did, Japanese Americans received very little pay for their efforts.

hardship in selling personal possessions, homes, and businesses at a loss before leaving for camp, and many struggled to meet their outside obligations. Some, for example, were trying to make mortgage payments on farms that were being tended by others. Parents had trouble raising enough money to pay for items their children needed, such as shoes and clothes.

The work program was not a complete failure, however. Japanese Americans worked in every department of camp administration, including the mess halls, the recreation centers, camp police and maintenance departments, health and sanitation, construction, plumbing, teaching, and agriculture. The WRA estimated that by the end of 1943 the camps were producing 85 percent of the vegetables used in camp and had sold to the outside world another 2.5 million pounds (1.1 million kg) of vegetables. Some camps raised hogs, chickens, and cattle, and a few developed dairies, offering fresh milk and cream. Manzanar organized a camp-wide project that produced camouflage nets used by the military, and other camps had sawmills, sewing projects, and woodworking programs.

The camp newspapers that thrived at every center, such as the *Tulean Dispatch* and the *Manzanar Free Press*, were a source of pride. Supervised by a WRA employee, the publications appeared anywhere from daily at Poston to weekly or twice a week at the other camps. The papers informed the internees of developments inside the camp as well as elsewhere throughout the world. They printed public announcements, listed the dances and other activities for the coming week, and published other information to assist the Japanese Americans in adjusting to difficult times.

Japanese Americans viewed these publications as a powerful way of quietly protesting the unfair treatment to which they had been subjected and as an affirmation that, even from behind barbed wire, the Bill of Rights existed. As long as they had the right to publish their opinions, even if overly critical comments were censored by administrators, they held onto at least a portion of those freedoms guaranteed to everyone in a democracy and were reminded with each edition that greater freedoms awaited them at some point in the future.

Education

A major concern for Japanese American parents was the education of their children, who were unable to attend public or private schools along with the rest of the nation while they were in camp. The WRA planned to develop an educational system, but when the evacuees arrived, little was in place. "With no exceptions, schools at the centers opened in unpartitioned barracks meant for other purposes and generally bare of furniture," stated a government report on the internment camps. "Sometimes the teacher had a desk and chair; more often she had only a chair. In the first few weeks many of the children had no desks or chairs and for the most part were obliged to sit on the floor—or stand up all day."[69]

Eleanor Gerard Sekerak volunteered to teach at Topaz because she wanted to help young Japanese Americans. She instructed her high school students from a hastily assembled barracks with benches and a pot-bellied stove. As many as eighty students jammed into some barracks, often sitting on the floor and using outdated equipment. Teachers collected whatever materials they could scrounge. One instructor in a typing class at Tule Lake lacked typewriters, so she told her students to draw circles on paper to rep-

Students listen to their instructor during a science lesson at Manzanar Relocation Center. Japanese American children were still required to attend school, even though they could not go to public school. Their classrooms were made from unpartitioned barracks, and they had very few resources.

resent the keyboard and had them practice with that makeshift remedy.

"In the beginning, faculty meetings were an exercise in how to tolerate frustration, as we wrestled with the 'how to' of a core curriculum in a community school with few supplies and practically no library," said Sekerak. She had such few supplies that she contacted the teachers with whom she had worked in Oakland, California, for help, and they promptly mailed old textbooks to their friend. When her students complained about using old textbooks, Sekerak replied, "History is history, government is government. You don't need a brand-new book!"[70]

Conditions gradually improved as more up-to-date materials arrived. New desks replaced benches, and laboratories that started without microscopes or other crucial items eventually operated with at least partial supplies.

Schools constantly struggled to find qualified teachers. Camp volunteers lacked certification, and the ones

Parent-Child Relationships

Some observers claimed that the internment camps helped break down the close ties that bound Japanese American families. While much evidence exists to support that contention, others countered that it did no such thing and believe it had more to do with the normal parent-child relationship. Frank Bunya, who was a teenager during his internment, said that he and his friends did not need their parents as much in the camps because they were more on their own and did not need any money. He explains, "The family didn't really break down. Children just had a little more independence, that's all. The family didn't fall apart. A lot of parents were worried that it would. They were so used to being the dominant figures in the household. They feared we would just turn about face and become rabble-rousers, and cause lots of trouble, but that never happened."

Quoted in Audrie Girdner and Anne Loftis. *The Great Betrayal*. London: Macmillan, 1969, p. 314.

A Japanese American family stays close to one another while they wait to be evacuated. Some feel that the internment camps damaged the traditional ties of Japanese American families.

who possessed a college degree were normally those from the outside like Sekerak, dedicated teachers who hoped to help improve a dismal situation or show Japanese Americans that not every white American considered them traitors. A group of Maryknoll nuns, a Catholic religious order, taught at Manzanar.

The camps offered a full curriculum to the students, from nursery schools through high school and adult education. They had to match the educational requirements for the state in which they operated, providing for instruction in the core subjects, such as mathematics and history, as well as extracurricular activities, such as clubs, class yearbooks, chorus, student newspaper, student government, drama, athletics, and dances. The graduating high school classes at Topaz borrowed caps and gowns from the University of Utah so they could march to their ceremony in formal attire.

At Poston a former actor organized a drama group and the University of Chicago gave college credit for certain classes. The University of California, Los Angeles (UCLA) offered extension courses at Manzanar, which also established a junior college recognized by the state's Department of Education. Adult classes in English, drafting, and other subjects helped older Japanese Americans and tried to prepare them for life after the war.

The students and teachers noticed the strange irony that marked their school days. It was awkward for many to daily mutter the Pledge of Allegiance to a nation that forced them to leave homes and friends. Sekerak struggled with the quandary of imparting U.S. history and government to students who could look out the windows and see guards and watchtowers. "As I faced my first day I wondered how I could teach American government and democratic principles while we sat in classrooms behind barbed wire!"[71] she wrote. Students smirked in some classes when the teacher began lessons covering the Bill of Rights, and Ruth Fischer, who taught at Tule Lake, cried as she graded her students' essays on the topic, "The Saddest Day of My Life." Each one had chosen the same moment— the evacuation from their homes.

Teachers struggled to instruct students who, knowing their former friends enjoyed the complete benefits and diverse programs offered in outside schools, adopted an apathetic attitude. Teachers in camps cited low morale among students, who wondered why they needed a good education to live in a nation that did not want them, as a chief issue. The outstanding educators, like Sekerak, faced the problem head-on by discussing it with their students and reminding them that while they had the right to feel sorry for themselves, if they failed to gain an education now, then they would suffer worse conditions when the camps one day closed. Sekerak's students came to class on time, homework complete, ready to learn.

No matter how dedicated the teacher or how modern the equipment, students confined against their will operated at a disadvantage that did not exist outside the camps. Many overcame the problem through simple hard work and determination, but others struggled to attain the levels of knowledge they might have achieved if they had remained in their communities along the West Coast.

Sports and Other Activities

Internees fought a constant battle against boredom. Cut off from the usual activities in the outside world, they turned to WRA-sponsored endeavors, but the government organization was again caught in its familiar quandary: It wanted to provide sports, dances, and other events but had to be cautious lest critics attack it for making camp life too pleasant.

Social activities, such as glee clubs, dances, concerts, Boy Scouts, and Girl Scouts, were prominent in each camp. Chess and checkers vied with card games and art competitions, and some camps offered movie theaters featuring the latest Hollywood films. Like the rest of the country, camps organized Red Cross blood drives, scrap metal drives, and bond sales to aid the war effort, and the Young Men's Christian Association (YMCA) and the Young Women's Christian Association (YWCA) opened chapters in every camp. Games and crafts helped pass the time, and on weekends some internees hiked beyond the fence to mountain or desert sites the WRA had approved in advance. Younger internees especially loved listening to radio stations playing the current hit songs but wildly jeered or turned away in disgust whenever the popular 1944 Bing Crosby song, "Don't Fence Me In," aired.

Many internees participated in musicals, singing performances, and stage plays. The Jerome Camp in Arkansas organized a Fourth of July program to honor the nation's independence, which included speakers reciting President Abraham Lincoln's renowned Gettysburg Address while standing in front of a large picture of the Civil War leader and an American flag. Some in the audience were moved to tears by the presentation, but others reacted angrily to a celebration of independence while they were detained behind barbed wire. "It didn't make sense, but it was our hearts' cry," said Mary Tsukamoto of the event. "We wanted so much to believe that this was a government by the people and for the people and that there was freedom and justice."[72]

Daisuke Kitagawa, who spent his war years at Tule Lake, wrote an essay about one Fourth of July program, explaining what the events meant to his fellow Japanese Americans:

> We dare celebrate the Fourth of July even in this place because we complied with the evacuation order to show our patriotism to this nation. Others are showing their patriotism in other ways. Unfortunately ours had to take this form of expression. Nevertheless, our being here is no less an evidence of our loyalty to the USA than going to war is with others. So it is as loyal citizens of the USA that we are going to celebrate the Fourth of July.[73]

Most camps had libraries—Manzanar had five branches in all—and offered classes in making crepe-paper flowers, gardening, music, needlework, judo, and a host of other activities. Baseball, football, and basketball teams, such as the Manzanar Giants and the Terminal Island Termites, vied with each other for league championships before enthusiastic crowds, and one camp pitted one hundred baseball squads in an elaborate tournament. Ping-Pong, judo, boxing, and badminton contests flourished at other centers.

Even though the camps offered weekly dances and other social events for teenagers and young adults, a lack of privacy made dating harder than it was outside the fences. High school males and females wanted to mingle like normal youths, but they were confined in close proximity to their parents and other people. Enterprising boys and girls came up with their own solutions for privacy, but they always risked being interrupted by an adult or friend.

Japanese Americans tried to duplicate as many of their normal activities as possible in an effort to retain a connection with the outside world. They differed from other Americans simply because they looked so much like the Japanese enemy, but they responded to the same music, the same dances, and the same emotions as any other American.

Peter Simpson learned this firsthand. A white teenager living in Cody, Wyoming, near the Heart Mountain Relocation Center, he was at first uneasy with the proximity of so many Japanese Americans and was happy that military police and barbed wire shielded him from the internees. One day his Episcopal minister, John McGlaughlin, took him and some other boys to the camp for a religious service. Simpson's apprehension increased as he passed through the gate and entered "an absolutely alien, strange, horrifying, and difficult world."[74]

The group headed to the recreation hall for the service, where Simpson watched the internees arrive. As they filtered in, he discovered a startling fact. "Not only did everybody there speak the same language I did, they actually knew the service better than I did."[75]

The revelation that he had things in common with Japanese Americans changed Simpson. "After that Sunday, it was never quite as easy to fit the people of the Heart Mountain Relocation Center into the stereotype of the enemy abroad."[76]

Simpson returned to the camp three more times in one year, each time deepening the friendships he formed with

Onlookers watch a baseball game underway at an internment camp. Life in the camps included many social activities to help fill the time. People at the camps attended dances, plays, and concerts as well as playing games such as chess.

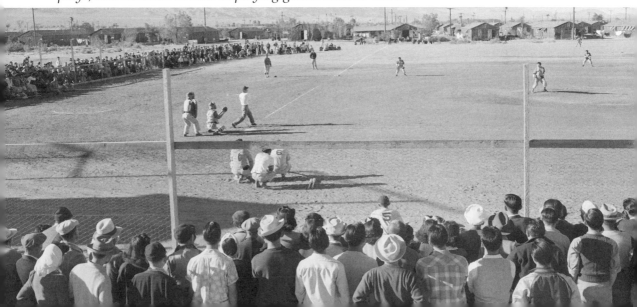

The Ability to Endure

James A. Michener, a Pulitzer Prize–winning author of more than forty books of fiction, praised the Japanese American ability to quietly endure as the world about them and all they cherished were being stripped away after Japan attacked Pearl Harbor. In the introduction to the book *Years of Infamy: The Untold Story of America's Concentration Camps*, written by Michi Nishiura Weglyn, Michener writes, "The stark heroism with which the impounded Japanese Americans behaved after their lives had been torn asunder and their property stolen from them must always remain a miracle of American history. The majesty of character they displayed then and the freedom from malice they exhibit now should make us all humble."

James A. Michener. Introduction to *Years of Infamy: The Untold Story of America's Concentration Camps*, by Michi Nishiura Weglyn. New York: Morrow, 1976, p. 31.

Japanese American youths. "The distance between Cody and Heart Mountain was twelve-and-one-half miles, but it seemed like the longest trip in the world for a young boy between two cultures and two separate times."[77]

Family and Faith

The WRA allowed the Japanese Americans to help run each camp through community councils, but in doing so it inadvertently created tension among the internees. The government specified that only U.S. citizens could participate on the councils and that created conflict between the Issei and the Nisei. The Issei, who were not citizens, saw their traditional leadership role in the community and within their own families weaken.

Other aspects of camp life diminished the importance of family that marked the Japanese way of life. Rather than remaining together for activities, especially dinner, younger people rushed to mess halls to eat with their friends, devoured their meals, and left before their parents arrived. The elderly or infirm could not walk great distances for their meals, meaning that someone had to bring their food to the barracks. It was possible for teenagers to go through an entire day hardly seeing their parents, which was almost unheard of before camp existence. The family unit that had been so cherished dissolved under the stress of internment. "My own family, after three years of mess hall living, collapsed as an integrated unit,"[78] wrote Jeanne Wakatsuki Houston.

The father lost respect as the traditional strong figure in the family. His role as provider of food and other needs was supplanted by the U.S. government, and his ability to discipline was weakened by living in communal barracks lacking privacy. Young adults began to view their parents as powerless to affect matters. Since the parents also worked at occupations provided by the government for low wages, the children also began to realize that they were being taken care of by people outside the family unit. "Caucasian people governed and Japanese people were governed,"[79] wrote Kitagawa of his time at Tule Lake.

In the midst of such tribulations, Japanese Americans turned to their faith to help them endure. The WRA allowed Japanese Americans to practice any religion of their choosing, except for Shinto, because that religion involves worshipping the Japanese emperor. Each camp offered one building, normally the recreation hall or one of the barracks, for services, and internees could invite pastors from outside the camp to conduct services. Catholic, Methodist, Presbyterian, Episcopalian, Baptist, and

A community council meeting is in session at Manzanar Relocation Center. Japanese Americans helped the WRA run the camps through community councils, but not everyone was happy with this arrangement. The government only allowed citizens to participate.

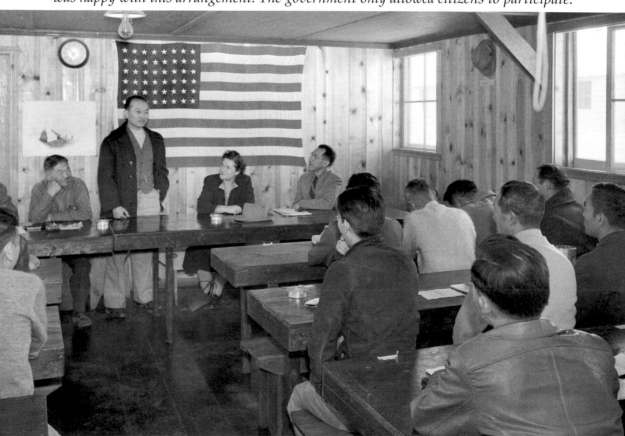

Buddhist ceremonies tended enthusiastic worshippers, while Sunday school classes ministered to the youth. At Manzanar, Maryknoll nuns even operated an orphanage.

In addition to their faith, the Issei had a sense of discipline and acceptance of hardship that helped them process the numerous demands that chipped away at their way of life. The family unit may have been dissolving, but many parents endured with the intent of emerging as stronger individuals because of it.

Early in her internment Gruenewald complained to her mother that she and every other Japanese American had been tricked into going along with the evacuation. "I thought every American citizen was supposed to have life, liberty, and the pursuit of happiness," Gruenewald explained. "That's what we were told in school back home, but that isn't what we have here." Her mother replied that times were hard for everyone and that they needed to be patient. "Twenty years from now," said her mother, whom Gru-

Japanese Americans in an internment center gather with their priest in front of their makeshift church. Camp residents were allowed to practice almost any religion. Faith helped many people endure the difficult days.

enewald credited with being the foundation of her family, "we may have nothing more than the memories of how we conducted ourselves with dignity and courage during this difficult time. What kind of memories do we want to have then of how we faced these difficulties now?" Her mother advised Gruenewald to quietly accept the way things were and to make each day the best she could. Eventually, she reminded Gruenewald, the ordeal would end and they would resume their lives. "Quietly accepting the order to evacuate was a survival technique," wrote Gruenewald of her mother. "Resistance didn't seem like an option."[80]

Whenever Houston moaned about conditions at Manzanar, her parents admonished, "We're here, and there's no use moaning about it forever."[81]

Early in her confinement at Topaz, Toyo Suyemoto complained about every restriction and about what she was missing in the outside world. His mother replied, "Spring will come again." When Suyemoto answered, "But it won't be the same spring," her mother said, "No, not the same spring, but another spring, a new spring."[82] In other words, hang on, endure, and things will one day improve.

A reporter for the *Chicago Daily Tribune* studied some of the internment camps and concluded that the Japanese American ability to endure was a chief reason why they successfully handled difficult times. "But one of the most important factors in that orderly exodus of 110,000 men, women, and children," concluded the reporter, "was the general acceptance by the Japanese of a hard decision and their determination to make the best of an extremely bad situation."[83]

Although many Japanese Americans accepted the internment, others did not. Riots and court cases kept the issue on the front pages of newspapers across the country.

Chapter Five

Protesting the Internment

By forcibly interning such large numbers of people, the U.S. government created a situation where, sooner or later, emotions were certain to erupt in one fashion or another. Tensions slowly built, needing only a spark to pit person against person and internees against authorities.

Early Eruptions

Each time that unrest erupted in one of the camps, even if minor, the American public condemned it as a traitorous act by pro-Japanese internees. While that was accurate in a few cases, most of the disruptions occurred because of the severe conditions in which the Japanese Americans lived or as a response to having their rights violated.

Some protested against the Japanese American Citizens League (JACL), the organization that, in an effort to avoid bloodshed, urged Japanese Americans to accept the internment as a sign of

their loyalty to the United States. "I kind of thought we were going too much like sheep,"[84] said Paul Shinoda of his confinement at Amache in Colorado. He and others believed they should have been more vocal in their displeasure.

Some believed that JACL leaders received favors from camp administrators. Others accused JACL leaders of secretly delivering the names of protesters to camp administrators, while the JACL fired back that the protesters were being disloyal to the United States. Members of a group called the Black Dragons at Manzanar threw rocks at internees who crafted camouflage nets for the U.S. military and beat up those they believed collaborated with the camp administration.

Other arguments flared between internees who had moved into the camps first and those who arrived later. The people who arrived later contended that the initial arrivals had grabbed all the best jobs. Later in the war, when the military began accepting Japanese Americans, eighty-five internees refused induction into the military, asking why they should fight and possibly die for a nation that so readily took away their rights. A federal grand jury indicted the men, who eventually received three-year jail terms in federal penitentiaries.

Demonstrations occurred the few times that camp guards shot internees. At Topaz, a guard, thinking that a man was attempting to escape, erroneously shot and killed an elderly internee who had wandered too close to the fence. Another guard at Gila River wounded a mentally deranged man when he did the same.

At Poston in November 1942 a group of internees beat another internee suspected of cooperating with camp administration. When authorities arrested two men, a crowd of one thousand gathered to demand their release, and a leadership committee called for a general strike that halted camp work. The strike ended when the administration agreed to free one man and release the other into the custody of a lawyer until his trial.

Incident at Manzanar

The most serious incident occurred at Manzanar, where bitter feelings split the camp into pro-Japanese and pro-U.S. factions. On December 5, 1942, Fred Tayama, a JACL official, was badly beaten by six internees for his supposed cooperation with camp administrators. When he identified one of his attackers, camp police quickly arrested the individual. The next day a group of pro-Japanese internees stormed into the hospital looking for Tayama, but doctors hid him under a bed, and the angry dissidents left without locating their target.

At about the same time another incident was occurring. When Harry Ueno noticed that sugar and meat—two items that were in great demand outside the camps due to wartime shortages—had been disappearing, he mentioned it at a block managers' meeting and demanded that steps be done to halt the disappearance. Authorities arrested Ueno for causing a disturbance.

Later in the day a crowd gathered to protest the arrests of Ueno and the individual charged with attacking Tayama. Ralph Merritt, the camp administrator, called in the military police (MP) who, supported by machine guns, arrived with bayonets attached to their rifles. The crowd grew angrier and began shouting insults at the young MPs. When the crowd refused to disband, the MPs shot tear gas into the group, but once the gas blew away, the crowd again gathered. More harsh words were exchanged, and a sergeant standing in front of his MPs glared at the crowd. "Now, I hope you Japs do something," he barked at the demonstrators as he brandished his .45 pistol. "I'd sure like to use this on you."[85]

Hostile feelings intensified. Even though the officer in charge did not give an order to fire, some of the young guards, unnerved by what they witnessed, fired into the crowd, killing two persons and wounding another nine.

Fred Tayama, third from left, chairman of the Japanese American Citizens League (JACL), speaks with Los Angeles mayor Fletcher Bowron in 1941. A year later, Tayama was badly beaten at Manzanar. The camp divided into pro-Japanese and pro-United States political feelings, and as a JACL leader, Tayama became a target for the pro-Japanese faction.

The protesters dispersed, but camp authorities arrested those they suspected of leading the affair and eventually relocated them to other government camps to separate them from their compatriots in Manzanar. An investigation into the disappearance of sugar and meat later determined that a camp official had been stealing the food. He was loading the goods into the trunk of his car, driving out of camp, and selling them outside for a huge profit.

Three Court Cases

Three Japanese Americans turned to the court system to challenge the U.S. government's right to evacuate and intern Japanese Americans. Gordon K. Hirabayashi, a senior at the University of Washington, refused to register for the evacuation. On May 16, 1942, Hirabayashi, accompanied by his lawyer, Arthur Barnett, turned himself in to the Federal Bureau of Investigation (FBI) in Seattle. Hirabayashi explained in a paper he handed to the agents that, as a Quaker, he opposed violence and that the evacuation "forces thousands of energetic, law-abiding individuals to exist in a miserable psychological and a horrible physical atmosphere. This order limits to almost full extent the creative expression of those subjected. It kills the desire for a higher life. Hope for the future is exterminated." He added that if he registered, he would then be agreeing with the evacuation, which would be a "denial of practically all of the things which give me incentive to live." Due to his religious beliefs, he had a duty to object, and he stated, "I must refuse this order for evacuation."[86]

Hirabayashi and his lawyer wanted to send the issue into the court system, where they hoped that a judge would rule against the evacuation. His case, *Hirabayashi v. United States*, eventually worked its way up to the highest court in the land, the U.S. Supreme Court in Washington, D.C., and in June 1943 the Court ruled 9–0 in favor of the government, noting that it had done nothing unconstitutional in singling out Japanese Americans for evacuation. The Court also noted in its decision that "residents having ethnic affiliations with an invading enemy may be a greater source of danger than those of different ancestry,"[87] and that it was not the responsibility of the Supreme Court to doubt the nation's military in deciding who posed a threat to the country's safety during wartime. Justice Frank Murphy, however, wrote that while the court agreed with the government, the evacuation

was disturbingly similar to Nazi Germany's treatment of Jewish citizens leading up to and during the war.

The Supreme Court ruled on the two other cases the following year. In May 1942 authorities arrested Fred T. Korematsu as he walked with his girlfriend in San Leandro, California. Whereas Hirabayashi challenged the evacuation in court, Korematsu simply ignored the evacuation order. "I figured I'd lived here all my life and I was going to stay here,"[88] he explained.

In December 1944 the Court again sided with the government, 6–3, in *Korematsu v. United States*, approving the evacuation as a military necessity. In the majority opinion Justice Hugo L. Black wrote that the evacuation was not ideal, but "when under conditions of modern warfare our shores are threatened by hostile forces, the power to protect must be commensurate with the threatened danger." He added, "We are unable to conclude that it was beyond the war powers of Congress and of the Executive [the president of the United States] to exclude those of Japanese ancestry from the West Coast area at the time they did." Justice Black agreed that Korematsu suffered hardship, "but hardships are part of war, and war is an aggregation of hardships. All citizens alike, in uniform and out of uniform, feel the impact of war in greater or lesser measure."[89]

Justices Owen J. Roberts, Frank Murphy, and Robert H. Jackson dissented on the grounds that the government had violated the Constitution and that its actions against Korematsu could not be justified by military reasons. Murphy ruled that the exclusion "goes over the very brink of constitutional power and falls into the ugly abyss of racism. No reasonable relations to an immediate, imminent and impending public danger is evident to support this racial restriction which is one of the most sweeping and complete deprivations of constitutional rights in the history of this nation in the absence of martial law."[90]

The third case, *Ex parte Mitsuye Endo*, singled out the internment as unconstitutional rather than the evacuation. Japanese American Mitsuye Endo was a Methodist, her parents had never returned to Japan, she neither read nor spoke Japanese, and her brother served in the U.S. Army. Her lawyers told her to report to her internment camp as ordered, and then in June 1942 they filed a petition asking the government to explain why Endo should not be released.

Gordon Hirabayashi, right, speaks to the media in 1983, along with two other Japanese Americans whose cases from the 1940s were reopened. Hirabayashi was a student in 1942 and refused to register for evacuation. He took his case to court, but the courts ruled that the U.S. government had done nothing illegal in ordering Japanese Americans to evacuate.

This Is Our Country

The loyalty issue split the Japanese Americans confined in the camps into two groups. Some who refused to answer no to the loyalty question decided to renounce (give up) their U.S. citizenship and return to Japan. Sergeant Tatsumi Iwate, who suffered a wound to the brain while fighting the German army during the war, was disappointed that a friend of his interned in a camp chose to renounce his U.S. citizenship. In a letter to his friend he wrote, "I am rather disappointed because you have lost faith in your country. I'm an American to the last drop of my blood. Being a person of Japanese descent, I'm aware of discrimination that is practiced by people who dare not see further than the color of our skin, but I'm very proud and I'll continue to fight the enemy of our country, be it foreign or domestic."

Quoted in *New York Times*. "Nisei GI Pleads for U.S.," July 16, 1945.

Like the others, Endo's case worked its way up to the Supreme Court, where the judges unanimously sided with Endo. Justice William O. Douglas stated, "Loyalty is a matter of the heart and mind, not of race, creed or color." Justice Murphy claimed the internment was "another example of the unconstitutional resort to racism inherent in the entire evacuation program" and that it was "utterly foreign to American ideals and traditions."[91]

The *Endo* ruling prodded the government to hasten the release and incorporation of Japanese Americans into normal society. The government announced that it would, hopefully, close the camps within a year. It asked citizens, especially those on the West Coast, to set aside harsh feelings and welcome the Japanese Americans as they attempted to rebuild their lives.

Support for an All-Japanese Military Unit

In January 1943 the government announced the formation of an all-Nisei army combat unit. This set in motion a chain of events that led to both the creation of one of the military's most acclaimed regiments as well as a major controversy that left Japanese Americans confused and frustrated. The rioting at Manzanar, combined with the need to find loyal men to serve, prodded the government into determining which Japanese Americans could be considered loyal to the United States and which were disloyal and should be separately confined.

At first the government banned all Japanese Americans from the military. On the war's first day about five thousand Nisei from Hawaii and the mainland were already serving in the army, but draft boards quickly stopped drafting Japanese Americans. The War Department announced that it would release most of those currently serving and would no longer accept Japanese Americans for military service except for a handful of men fluent in Japanese to translate captured enemy documents and do other work in gathering intelligence.

Momentum to admit Japanese Americans into the military began building shortly afterward, however. In October 1942 Elmer Davis, the director of the Office of War Information (OWI), suggested to President Roosevelt that the government needed to counter Japanese claims of discrimination. "Japanese propaganda to the Philippines, Burma, and elsewhere insists that this is a racial war. We can combat this effectively with counter propaganda only if our deeds permit us to tell the truth."[92] Davis argued that the nation could hardly boast of fighting for democracy while

Nisei troops in the U.S. Army are honored for their service during World War II by President Harry S. Truman in 1946. An all-Nisei army combat unit was formed by the U.S. government in 1943 and fought in Europe. Japanese Americans were conflicted about this opportunity to serve a government that had forced them out of their homes and into uncomfortable camps.

denying the right to fight to an entire group of people.

Assistant secretary of war John McCloy sent Colonel William P. Scobey to visit some of the camps. Scobey concluded that most Japanese Americans favored an all-Nisei unit, which would give their young men an opportunity to show their loyalty by fighting for the United States and risking their lives. "The Army had said that Nisei protestations of loyalty were so much hogwash," said internee Mike Masaoke. "We had to have a demonstration in blood."[93]

By November 1942 the JACL was campaigning for such a unit. The organization claimed that Japanese Americans were as loyal to the United States as any ethnic group and that many young men in the camps were bitter that they had been denied entrance to the army. President Roosevelt joined in two months later by writing to his secretary of war, Henry Stimson, "No loyal citizen of the United States should be denied the right to exercise the responsibilities of his citizenship regardless of his ancestry. The principle on which this country was founded and by which it has always been governed is that Americanism is a matter of mind and heart; Americanism is not, and never was, a matter of race or ancestry."[94]

Although the navy, the bulk of whose forces served in the Pacific, continued to ban Japanese Americans, claiming that their presence posed a problem not present in the European conflict, government officials decided to open the army to Japanese Americans. To do so, they first had to determine which internees were loyal to the United States and which retained a deep loyalty to the Japanese emperor. They also concluded that if the government opened the military to Japanese Americans, it could hardly refuse to allow Japanese Americans to aid the war effort in other ways.

The Loyalty Questionnaire

To help it determine who could leave camp for either service in the army or for another occupation, the government designed a questionnaire for internees to complete. Certain questions on the questionnaire unintentionally created confusion and anger among Japanese Americans.

In February 1943 ten teams of army and WRA personnel arrived at the camps to administer the questionnaire. They received a chilly response from internees at most camps. The internees had endured waves of hardship since Pearl Harbor and were insulted that the government now wanted to test their loyalty.

Two questions in particular bothered the internees. Question 27 asked draft-age males, "Are you willing to serve in the armed forces of the United States on combat duty, wherever ordered?" Question 28 focused on the loyalty issue by asking, "Will you swear unqualified allegiance to the United States of America and faithfully defend the United States from any or all attack by foreign or domestic forces, and forswear any form of allegiance or obedience to the Japanese emperor, or any other foreign government, power or organization?"[95]

Other Forced Evacuations

Although the United States received worldwide attention for its massive intern-ment of Japanese Americans during World War II, other nations in the Western Hemisphere adopted similar programs, albeit on a smaller scale. Canada removed from its Pacific coast all Japanese male aliens aged eighteen to sixty-five and placed them in work camps. The Mexican government moved Japanese living in Baja California to the mainland, while the governments in Peru and Colombia placed Japanese aliens under surveillance.

Respondents did not know how to answer the questions. If they replied that they would forswear allegiance to the Japanese emperor, then did that mean that they admitted they had been loyal to him? If they denounced Japanese nationality but were not already American citizens, as was the case for many Issei, would they be people without a country? If they answered no to either question, would they be considered disloyal, even though the reason for their answer might be due to a desire to remain with ailing family or for some other innocent reason?

Others hesitated to answer yes to Question 27 because they were angry their government had confined them to camps, or they had dependents to care for in camp, or they feared being sent into combat against relatives from Japan. Would the government interpret a yes to Question 27 as an indication the man wanted to volunteer for military service? If a person enlisted, would their families

be targeted by groups of angry Japanese Americans who threatened reprisals to those who said yes?

Mary Matsuda Gruenewald, who had been born in the United States, was irritated that her government wanted to know whether she was loyal to an emperor about whom she knew little. How could she be a saboteur, Gruenewald wondered, if she was confined behind barbed wire fences? Would her family be split apart if they answered differently? Some friends cautioned that if she answered yes to both questions, then she would be forced to leave the camp, while others were equality insistent that Gruenewald had to answer yes to get her rights back. If she answered yes, would that help send her brother to war and to his possible death? "In their haste to get the registration underway quickly, the WRA had thrust every interned family onto the horns of a terrible dilemma," wrote Gruenewald. "No matter what I do, it seemed like a no-win situation."[96]

Jeanne Wakatsuki Houston said that in Manzanar the "very idea of the oath itself became the final goad that prodded many once-loyal citizens to turn militantly anti-American."[97] Gangs of incensed Japanese Americans roamed some camps, warning people to reply no and threatening those who answered yes. "I had never been so terrified in my life," claimed Gruenewald of the hectic time at Tule Lake. "Suddenly I was hated not just by my government but by other Japanese Americans."[98]

A government report completed in 1982 concluded that in its haste to determine who was loyal and who was disloyal, the government created chaos and bitterness instead of order. "The resulting infighting, beatings, and verbal abuses left families torn apart, parents against children, brothers against sisters, relatives against relatives, and friends against friends. So bitter was all this that even to this day, there are many amongst us who do not speak about that period for fear that the same harsh feelings might arise up again to the surface."[99]

Reasons for Answers

In the end, most internees answered yes to Question 27 and Question 28, especially in those camps where government administrators had developed good relations with the Japanese Americans. At Minidoka, the administrator met with Japanese American leaders before calling for a camp-wide gathering so he would be better prepared to know what to say to the internees. Japanese Ameri-

can leaders, including Issei, participated in the meeting and helped clear up any doubts before the questionnaires were administered. As a result, Minidoka had more yes answers than any other camp. The administrator at Tule Lake, on the other hand, convened a brief meeting that allowed no time for discussion. That camp saw more no answers than any other location.

Gruenewald's family, trusting that the United States would soon end their ordeal, ignored the threats and answered yes to both questions. Her brother answered yes even if it meant induction into the army, asserting that in doing so he was proving his loyalty to the nation. "Although I knew 'Yes Yes' was the right choice," wrote Gruenewald, "it broke my heart. I felt like giving in to the bully in the schoolyard."[100] Gruenewald claimed she answered yes more from a sense of devotion to her family rather than from a sense of loyalty to the United States. After everyone finished the questionnaires, Gruenewald's brother told them to keep their decision quiet to avoid being harassed by others.

According to a survey conducted by the WRA, 87 percent of all internees answered yes to the loyalty question. The 13 percent who answered no or renounced their citizenship were classified as disloyal, even though for the majority the answer had little to do with loyalty.

On July 6, 1943, the U.S. Senate adopted a resolution ordering the WRA to confine those who answered no to Tule Lake. Starting in September 1943, the WRA transferred 6,538 people out of Tule Lake, including Gruenewald's family, and into Heart Mountain and moved 12,173 to Tule Lake from other camps, including George Takei's family. The WRA erected a double 8-foot (2.4m) fence, increased the number of guards, mounted machine guns in the guard towers, and stationed six tanks along the outer limits as a warning to those interned.

The overreaction by the government angered the internees, although it did not surprise them. Tule Lake became a hotbed of protest. Those who had been living in the camp all along resented the newcomers, while the fresh arrivals chafed at the government's treatment of them. Protesters organized a strike of eight hundred farm workers in October that threatened the harvest after a farm truck overturned and killed an intern-

An armed American soldier stands guard at Tule Lake internment camp. The camp became known for its protests after the U.S. government insisted that Japanese Americans complete a loyalty questionnaire before they could serve in the military.

ee. When the protesters approached the camp administrator's home, the army swiftly moved in to restore order and began unannounced searches of barracks. The next month Japanese Americans paraded around Tule Lake with the Rising Sun flag of Japan prominently held high.

The confusion and anger created by the loyalty questions never dissipated. At the same time, however, Japanese American soldiers gained praise for their heroism on European and Pacific battlefields. As the war wound to an end and as Japanese American military heroes made headlines, the government heard a greater clamor for closing the ten camps.

Into the Military

Japanese American youth showed an amazing ability to ignore the tribulations of internment and come to the defense of the nation that took away many of the basic rights they had enjoyed before the war. Instead of angrily protesting the government's attempt to bring them into the military, most embraced it as a chance to assert their loyalty. While some Nisei declined to volunteer because they did not want to fight relatives who still lived in Japan or feared that the Japanese government would punish those relatives because they had volunteered, twelve hundred men from the camps and fifteen hundred from Hawaii signed on.

Masaoke wanted his children to have a better life and claimed that his willingness to fight and die would help "prove beyond all doubt that we who are Americans in spite of our Japanese faces are loyal to the land of our birth, even unto death."[101] George Aki, who also joined the military, said, "No matter what has happened in the past, America is still my country. This is where my children will be born and will grow up."[102]

When one colonel asked a Japanese American soldier why he wanted to fight when so many of his relatives languished in camp, the soldier showed the officer a letter he had received from his father. "My son, I am dying," wrote the father. "As you know, I have lived and am dying as a Japanese loyal to the Emperor. You, on the other hand, were born in the United States and brought up in the United States as an American. You are American. You have had all the advantages of education. On my deathbed, I command you to fight for the United States, and if need be to give your life for the United States."[103]

Two different Japanese American military units formed—the 442nd Regimental Combat Team from the mainland and the 100th Battalion from Hawaii. The 442nd, which trained in Mississippi, chose the phrase, "Go for Broke," as its motto, indicating the men's desire to give everything they had to defeat the enemy. Realizing that their fellow countrymen would closely follow their actions, they intended to show that Japanese Americans were as willing to defend their nation with their lives as anyone else. One soldier said during training, "We are anxious to show what real lovers of American democracy will do to preserve it. Our actions will speak for us more than words."[104] Sergeant Burt Tanaka said, "We are glad of this chance to show the world that descendants of Japanese are just as good, loyal American citizens as descendants of Italians and Germans, who also are over here fighting."[105]

Fighting the Enemy

Both units impressed their officers and other units when they entered combat. The 100th Battalion went into combat in 1943, taking part in rough fighting in North Africa and Italy, where captured German soldiers told interrogators they feared the Japanese because they never surrendered. The battalion earned the nickname the Purple Heart Battalion because so many men were wounded. The nickname comes from the name of a combat medal, the Purple Heart, that the United States awards to members of the armed forces who are wounded in combat.

The 442nd landed in Italy the next year and swiftly moved northward along the coast toward Rome until joining with the 100th Battalion, which then became part of the 442nd Regimental Combat Team. They battled German forces entrenched in the mountains of Italy and France, so impressing their commander, Lieutenant General Mark W. Clark, commander of the Fifth Army, that he awarded them a Presidential Unit Citation. "You are always thinking of your country before yourselves," the citation stated. "You have never complained through your long periods in the line. You have writ-

ten a brilliant chapter in the history of the fighting men in America. You are always ready to close with the enemy, and you have always defeated him. The 34th Division is proud of you, the Fifth Army is proud of you, and the whole United States is proud of you."[106]

In late October 1944 the unit came to the rescue of a battalion from Texas that had been cut off and surrounded by German forces in the Vosges Mountains in eastern France. Two rescue attempts had already failed when the 442nd was brought in, and in six days of bitter fighting in which it suffered 800 casualties, the unit broke through to reach the beleaguered battalion and save the 211 survivors.

Japanese Americans contributed in other ways. More than six thousand served in intelligence work, mostly in the Pacific, where they translated seized enemy documents and interrogated captured Japanese soldiers. The work might not have appeared as dangerous as what the 442nd did in Europe, but these men faced a peril their European counterparts did not—capture by a Japanese enemy who would without hesitation abuse them as traitors to the mother country.

"No group in the war had as much to lose," said the commander of the Allied Translator and Interpreter Section, Colonel Sidney F. Mashbir. "Capture would have meant indescribable horror to them and their relatives in Japan. They are worthy, as individuals and as a group, of the highest possible praise for their invaluable contribution to the success of Allied arms."[107]

Soldiers of the 100th Battalion arrive in the United States after duty in Europe. The 100th Battalion was the first all-Nisei unit to go into combat. Japanese Americans served with much courage and commitment during World War II, despite government concerns about their loyalty.

In translating captured enemy battle plans and other documents, Japanese Americans helped military commanders plan assaults or deflect enemy attacks. They uncovered a complete list of Japanese ships operating near Guadalcanal, an island in the South Pacific, and translated the enemy's naval plans to defend the Philippine Islands. In Burma, Sergeant Roy Matsumoto crawled close enough to the Japanese to overhear their battle plans. He returned to his unit with the information, then turned to the enemy and shouted in Japanese, "Charge, you soldiers of Japan, charge, charge, charge."[108] The enemy mounted an attack directly into American gunfire, which cut them down before they could do any harm.

The 442nd Regimental Combat Team and the 100th Battalion collected hundreds of medals. In seven major battles the 442nd suffered more than nine thousand casualties. It became the most decorated outfit in the army, and along with the 100th, its men received two Medals of Honor, the nation's highest military honor for bravery in combat; 350 Silver Stars; 810 Bronze Stars; and more than 3,000 Purple Hearts. Private First Class Sadao Munemori was awarded a Medal of Honor posthumously (after his death) for attacking and destroying two German machine gun nests by himself and then saving the men near him by jumping on a live hand grenade and smothering the blast with his body.

The 442nd became a superb propaganda tool for the U.S. government. Officials could argue that they handed Japanese Americans the same opportunity as any ethnic group in the United States to defend their nation, and WRA administrators used their exploits to gain wider acceptance for Japanese Americans leaving camps and relocating either to their former residences or to new locations.

When President Harry Truman, who assumed the presidency upon the death of Franklin Roosevelt in April 1945, awarded the 442nd Regimental Combat Team its Distinguished Unit Citation, he told the brave men, "You fought not only the enemy, but you fought prejudice, and you have won. Keep up that fight, and we continue to win—to make this great Republic stand for just what the Constitution says it stands for: the welfare of all the people all the time."[109]

Chapter Six

The End of Internment

The successes of Japanese American military regiments helped ease the internees' transition back into society. This unexpected outcome was good news for WRA administrators, whose goal from the beginning was to return Japanese Americans to life outside the camps and avoid establishing a segment of the population that indefinitely looked to the government for its sustenance and welfare.

Relocation Begins

In 1942 officials permitted individuals to temporarily leave camps to help harvest farm crops. By October 1942, ten thousand internees had taken advantage of the program, which got them outside the camps at least for a short period of time and allowed them to earn sorely needed cash. The success of this effort confirmed the government's belief that the public would accept the permanent relocation of Japanese Americans now that the military crisis had eased in the Pacific and the West Coast no longer appeared open to an invasion.

The WRA also arranged for college-age students to attend outside universities. A group of educators from the University of California, Berkeley sent a letter to President Roosevelt requesting such an arrangement, especially as the Japanese American community looked to these young men to be its future leaders. WRA administrator Milton Eisenhower enlisted the help of the American Friends Service Committee, which formed the National Student Relocation Council to assist young men and women in returning to college. This Quaker organization eventually helped forty-three hundred students enroll in various universities.

"I felt wonderful the day I left camp," said Helen Murao about leaving Minidoka for school in August 1943. When she arrived at the train station for her journey to Wisconsin, where a Presbyterian minister and his family sponsored her education, Murao purchased a Coke. The simple act moved the young woman, who had missed the ability to walk into a store and purchase whatever she wanted. Murao said that people can take their freedom for granted, "but if you've been deprived of it, it's very significant. When I ran in there as a teenager to buy that Coke, it was the freedom to buy it, the freedom to run out and do it."[110]

The success of both programs aided later efforts to relocate every Japanese American as soon as possible. Dillon Myer, who succeeded Eisenhower after he stepped down in June 1942, argued that his chief responsibility as head of the WRA was to dismantle the camps as quickly as possible. He believed the government faced an obligation to release loyal citizens without delay. He said that restricting Japanese Americans to camps produced bitter feelings among them and created a large group of people dependent on the government for its existence, neither of which was desirable. "Life in the centers is embittering many of the American-born Japanese," wrote a reporter for the *New York Times* in May 1943. After talking with internees, the reporter contended that confinement "is giving the elders the feeling that life is over for them and is causing a breakdown in the time-honored Japanese family tradition."[111]

At the end of 1943, attorney general Francis Biddle, the nation's top law enforcer, expressed his belief that the government could no longer delay relocation:

The important thing is to secure the re-absorption of about 95,000 Japanese, of whom two-thirds are citizens and who give every indication of being loyal to the United States, into normal American life. The present practice of keeping loyal American citizens in concentration camps on the basis of race for longer than is absolutely necessary is dangerous and repugnant to the principles of our Government. It is also necessary to act now so that the agitation against these citizens does not continue after the war.[112]

To assist people in relocation, which occurred over a period of months, the WRA established forty-two field offices around the country. These offices, which at first supervised the farm work program, attempted to create a favorable reception in the communities about to receive Japanese Americans and to locate jobs for the new arrivals. The offices worked closely with community resettlement committees and with church organizations to more smoothly integrate into society the men and women coming from the camps.

The Fear of Relocation

Many of the Japanese Americans, especially the older generation, feared leaving the camps. Internment might not have been the most enjoyable existence, but it had become familiar, and the internees had gotten to know one another. Outside, they faced uncertainty and possible rejection from people who had only a few years earlier shouted for their internment. Some wondered whether they could start over again. Others doubted that the bigotry of the war years and the racist newspaper headlines could ever be overcome. Unfounded rumors poured into every camp of hostile receptions experienced by those who had already left for the outside world.

The government gave each individual twenty-five dollars to cover the expenses of leaving camp and reestablishing themselves elsewhere. Many who returned to their former homes found them in poor condition or discovered that their possessions had been stolen or badly damaged. Cars were gone or stripped of valuable parts, weeds covered farms, and in a few cases returnees found strangers living in their former homes. Those who owned their land and homes before leaving for the camps fared better, especially those who formed agreements with friends and neighbors to take care of the property, but those who did not often had to look elsewhere for housing.

A Seattle barber proudly points to a sign above the cash register in his shop that warns "Japs" to keep away. Once the camps closed, Japanese Americans were allowed to return to their homes or go elsewhere, but they faced continued prejudice and discrimination from many other Americans.

Humiliation

The troubles for Japanese Americans did not end when they returned to society after being released from the internment camps. They often had to accept occupations that paid much less and carried less esteem than those they had had before internment. For many, the humiliation was an added burden. *Fortune* magazine wrote about such instances: "A doctor distinguished in his profession, who lived with grace and charm in a decently comfortable home before the war, is today huddled in a small room with all his family. He practices his profession for $19 a month at the center hospital serving under a Caucasian of lesser accomplishments, hired for considerably more money."

Fortune. "Issei, Nisei, Kibei." *Fortune*, April 1944, p. 74.

Protests greeted some of the returnees. New York City mayor Fiorello LaGuardia, who had raised no objections to the thousands of German and Italian American residing in New York, asked why his city should have to take the Japanese Americans that California and other West Coast states did not want. Tenants and property owners in Brooklyn Heights protested the establishment of a hostel to provide shelter for Japanese Americans, and five hundred citizens in New Jersey sought legal methods to remove five Japanese American farm laborers who relocated in their area.

People living along the West Coast feared that by emptying the ten camps, the WRA would create a stampede of Japanese Americans trying to return to former homes and would force people living on their farms or in their homes to suddenly leave. Farm organizations promised to do all they could to halt the return of so many people, which they argued would create a new wave of hatred along the coast. One irate farmer even suggested that Japanese supersubmarines prowled the Pacific coastline, waiting only for the return of their loyal Japanese from internment before striking.

The Hood River, Oregon, post of the American Legion struck from its honor roll the names of sixteen Japanese American soldiers who had fought in Europe, including one who had died in combat. The legion's national commander demanded that the names be restored, and the Portland Council of Churches condemned the move as a denial of those same rights for which every soldier fought, but five hundred Hood River citizens signed a newspaper advertisement affirming the post's decision. When the commander threatened to expel the Hood River post from the American Legion, the post reluctantly restored the names. "They had won their right to be there," stated the *New York Times*. "One of them had answered 'the question' [of loyalty] with his life."[113]

Japanese Americans encountered other issues as well. A severe housing shortage forced many to live in cramped quarters, and discrimination in the job market caused highly skilled workers to seek any job they could find, no matter how menial. Individuals who owned restaurants or other establishments before the war found it almost impossible to obtain bank loans to reopen.

Successes

Despite these obstacles, Japanese Americans slowly began to reintegrate themselves into different communities throughout the country and along the

Singer Frank Sinatra signs his autograph for members of an all-Nisei combat unit in 1946. Sinatra spoke up in support of Japanese American soldiers and encouraged the public to accept returning internees.

Bigotry in the Twenty-First Century

While many people hoped that the internment of Japanese Americans would become a cautionary tale against other such events, instances of hatred and misunderstanding toward minorities continued to occur into the twenty-first century. One example is how Arab Americans were treated by their follow Americans in the aftermath of the terrorist attacks on the United States on September 11, 2001.

In November 2011 the Learning Channel launched a new series titled *All American Muslim*. The show profiles Arab Americans in Dearborn, Michigan, a city that contains the largest Arab American community in the United States. The Florida Family Association, a group that defends what it considers values based on the Christian Bible, objected to the program, saying that the show undermines the United States. This group argued that "'All-American Muslim' is propaganda that riskily hides the Islamic agenda's clear and present danger to American liberties and traditional values." In their view, Islam's agenda is to destroy what the group considers the American way of life, one based upon Christian principles. In response to a letter it received from the Florida Family Association, national home improvement retailer Lowe's pulled its ads from the show.

The opposition left many in the Arab American community stunned. Cast member Suehaila Amen, a thirty-two-year-old judicial aide for the Dearborn District Court, said, "I'm saddened that any place of business would succumb to bigots and people trying to perpetuate their negative views on an entire community. This can happen to any member of a minority group. This country was not founded on hatred or racism. It was founded on inclusion and diversity."

Quoted in Oralandar Brand-Williams. "Lowe's Yanks Ads from 'All American Muslim.'" *Detroit News*, December 11, 2011.

Muslim Americans who appear on the television show All-American Muslim *speak at a panel discussion. Some people protested that it was Islamic propaganda, which shows that discrimination of minorities continues today.*

West Coast. First Lady Eleanor Roosevelt publicly announced her support of relocation, and crooner Frank Sinatra and comedian Bob Hope praised Japanese American soldiers and asked the nation to accept the internees.

Japanese Americans found warm welcomes in Chicago, Illinois, and in much of the Midwest. West Coast reluctance diminished when the feared flood of returnees failed to materialize, and people learned that they could continue their lives as normal. The Fish Cannery Workers Union in Monterey, California, announced that all five hundred of the Japanese American workers who had been part of the union before internment would be welcomed back to their old jobs and promised to help find lodging for those members.

Hostels in New York and other major cities provided temporary living quarters. Seabrook Farms in New Jersey hired fifteen hundred Japanese Americans, while New York hotels, including the famed Astor, Commodore, and Savoy Plaza, employed others. Secretary of the interior Harold Ickes hired Japanese American laborers to work his farm and urged his countrymen to do something similar. "I do not like the idea of loyal citizens, whatever their race or color, being kept in relocation centers any longer than need be,"[114] he said.

The Camps Close

As more individuals left, the government turned its efforts toward the permanent closing of all ten camps. In the spring of 1944 the War Department urged President Roosevelt to end the internment, and in June Secretary Ickes warned Roosevelt that the continued confinement of those people who had not yet left would be an injustice. Top military officials concluded that with the war's progress favoring the United States, no justification existed to keep Japanese Americans behind barbed wire. Roosevelt agreed, but fearing that the step might produce a backlash of protest from the West Coast states, he delayed announcing his decision until after the November 1944 presidential election.

Americans reelected President Roosevelt to a fourth term, and in December 1944 he canceled the internment policy. He announced that every Japanese American would be free to return to his or her home starting January 2, 1945, and that every camp would be closed within twelve months. To ease fears, the government issued a statement saying, "All persons of Japanese ancestry have been carefully examined and only those persons who have been cleared by military authority have been permitted to return. They should be accorded the same treatment and allowed to enjoy the same privileges accorded other law abiding American citizens or residents."[115] Japanese Americans who had avowed their loyalty to the emperor would be detained until they could either be returned to Japan or sent to other federal centers.

California governor Earl Warren asked his state's residents to accept the announcement and ordered police and public officials to develop joint plans

California governor Earl Warren encouraged residents of his state to accept the return of Japanese Americans released from the camps. He discouraged violence and discrimination.

to prevent violence. "I am sure," he remarked, "that all Americans will join in protecting constitutional rights of individuals involved and will maintain an attitude that will discourage friction and prevent civil disorder."[116]

The War Ends

As Japanese Americans gradually abandoned the ten camps, the United States attacked the Japanese homeland in stunning fashion. On August 6, 1945, it dropped an atomic bomb on Hiroshima, leveling the city. Three days later it dropped a second atomic bomb on Nagasaki, demolishing it. Japan surrendered on August 15.

George Watanabe heard the news over his radio at a New York City relocation center and shouted to the other residents, "It's over! It's over!"[117] They drank a toast to victory, then chatted about what might lie ahead for them. George Takei said news of the atomic bomb attacks stunned internees at Tule Lake. Many families had relatives living in one of the two cities. Mary Matsuda Gruenewald collapsed onto her bed upon learning the war had ended, cried, and thanked God that her ordeal was over. Jeanne Wakatsuki Houston stared at the photographs of the mushroom cloud erupting from Hiroshima after the bomb blast, realizing that her life had again been suddenly altered by a single military event. "This was as strange, as awesome, as mysteriously unnerving as Pearl Harbor had been. And in the same way that the first attack finished off one period in our lives, so this appalling climax marked the end of another." Although she and other Japanese Americans did not feel the same elation as the rest of the United States, Houston said, "At least we were no longer the enemy."[118]

All camps except Tule Lake closed by December 1945. Tule Lake shut down in early 1946. The WRA was finally dissolved in June 1946, and the evacuation and internment of Japanese Americans was over. They were no longer in the camps, but the effects lingered. "Now we faced a new anxiety," explained Takei, "the unknowns of life outside barbed wire confinement and stripped of everything."[119]

Returning Home

Japanese Americans experienced a mixture of reactions from other Americans. An unknown assailant fired six shotgun blasts into the home of one returning

The atomic bombing of Nagasaki resulted in a mushroom cloud in the air and widespread destruction of the city. The damage and death tolls from the bombings of both Hiroshima and Nagasaki quickly led to Japan's surrender.

Japanese American family near Fresno, California; one home was destroyed by fire; and signs cautioning Japanese Americans to stay away appeared in some locations. Generally, however, the reception was either friendly or one of uninterest.

Neighbors extended a rousing welcome on Vashon Island to Gruenewald's family, while Houston thought that people acted as if the internment had never happened and as if she and her family had never gone anywhere. The day that Patrick Hayashi's family was evacuated from their home and sent to camp, their neighbor uprooted some of the family's azaleas and kept them in bedding boxes. When the family returned three years later, the neighbor walked over with the flowers. "Here are your flowers," he said. "I've kept them for you so you can start your life again."[120]

Military veteran Wilson Makabe returned to Loomis, California, still showing evidence of the wounds he suffered in Italy the year before. He drove up to a gas station whose owner, earlier in the war, had posted signs saying, "No Jap trade wanted." The owner approached Makabe and said, with tears filling his eyes, "Now when I see you come back like that, I feel so small."[121]

Mitsuo Usui, wearing his military uniform and medals, boarded a California bus on his way home from the war. A woman sitting in the front row muttered, "Damn Jap" when she saw him. A stunned Usui did not know how to react, but the bus driver turned to the woman and said, "Lady, apologize to this American soldier or get off my bus." The woman refused and left the bus. The bus driver then said to a grateful Usui, "That's okay, buddy, everything is going to be okay from now on out."[122]

The bus driver correctly concluded that conditions would improve for Japanese Americans, but it was a slow process. In 1948 President Harry Truman signed a law that paid Japanese Americans for lost property, the same year that California voters defeated a bill that would have restricted ownership of land by Japanese Americans. In 1952 Japanese, including Issei, could become U.S. citizens, and by the next decade California's governor had appointed two Nisei lawyers, one of whom was escorted from his detention center in 1942 in order to take the bar examination, as judges. In 1971 Norman Mineta became the first Japanese American mayor of a major U.S. city outside Hawaii when voters in San Jose, California, elected him as their leader. Five years later President Gerald Ford officially ended the Japanese American internment when he rescinded Roosevelt's Executive Order 9066.

To Speak or Not

In the years following the war, most Japanese Americans declined to speak about their experiences. Some wanted to simply forget and move on, while others thought it was too painful to relive a terrible time. Parents were ashamed that they could not protect their children from what had occurred, and they urged their sons and daughters to blend in with American society rather than gen-

"A Square Deal"

From 1932 to 1942 Joseph Grew served as the U.S. ambassador to Japan. He had long argued against evacuation and internment of Japanese Americans and was an early voice advocating the hurried return of internees to regular society. In late 1943 Grew stated,

> I do know that like the Americans of German descent, the overwhelming majority of Americans of Japanese origin are wholly loyal to the United States. . . . It does not make for loyalty to be constantly under suspicion when grounds for suspicion are absent. I have too great a belief in the sanctity of American citizenship to want to see these Americans of Japanese descent penalized and alienated through blind prejudice. I want to see them given a square deal.

Quoted in *Time.* "Square Deal for the Japanese," November 29, 1943.

erate attention by asking about the war. Others declined to speak out because, no matter how horrible their treatment was, they knew that the terrors that Jewish families suffered in Nazi Germany's death camps during the war were much worse. Gruenewald felt guilt, as if she had committed a crime, and thus did not talk of her time in internment for years.

Feelings altered through the years as war passions cooled, and younger generations began asking about the internment. Donald Nakahata, who spent his war years in Topaz, said, "Simply to forget it and sweep it under the rug dishonors all those people whose lives were changed by it."[123]

Japanese Americans, supported by the Japanese American Citizens League (JACL), began seeking concessions from the U.S. government. At its 1978 national convention the JACL asked for an apology from the government and a cash payment of twenty-five thousand dollars for each person who had been placed in a camp. Three years later Senator Daniel Inouye of Hawaii, a Medal of Honor recipient, successfully pushed for the creation of the Commission on Wartime Relocation and Internment of Civilians (CWRIC). From July to December 1981, the commission heard testimony from hundreds of Japanese Americans. In its December 1982 report, *Personal Justice Denied*, the commission concluded that the internment was not justified and, rather than being executed due to military circumstances, it was carried out because of prejudice and hysteria.

Survivors walk through a German concentration camp, thin with starvation and suffering, their clothing in rags. After the war's end, many Japanese Americans did not speak about their experiences. They had mixed feelings about it. Some felt that they had not experienced treatment as horrible as the war's victims in Europe.

Consequently, Japanese Americans had suffered a grave injustice.

The committee made five recommendations. It called for an apology by the government, presidential pardons for those who were arrested for breaking laws when they resisted the evacuation or internment, restoration of status and entitlements lost because of the incarceration (such as veterans' benefits), the creation of a foundation to study the internment in an effort to avoid its repetition, and a tax-free payment of twenty thousand dollars to each survivor.

The Civil Rights Act of 1988 adopted all five recommendations. On August 10, 1988, President Ronald Reagan signed H.R. 442, so designated to honor the 442nd Regimental Combat Team, into law. The first letters of apology, signed by the president, went out in late 1989, with the first checks following in 1990. Payments were also sent out to the heirs of any former internees who had died before the bill became law.

Legal Issues and Discrimination

The court system followed suit, correcting injustices that had happened during the war. In April 1948 federal judge Louis E. Goodman ruled that those Japanese Americans who signed renunciation papers while at Tule Lake were to be restored as citizens. He said the government never should have accepted the papers because it was "fully aware of the coercion" they faced from pro-Japanese forces that caused the "fear, anxiety, hopelessness and despair of the renunciations."[124]

In January 1983 attorney Peter Irons filed a lawsuit in district court to reverse the criminal convictions of both Fred T. Korematsu and Gordon K. Hirabayashi. He claimed that the government purposely kept hidden from the court military and government reports proving that Japanese Americans in the early 1940s posed no military threat to the nation. Irons succeeded in both cases, with one judge ruling that the government in wartime has extra reason to be vigilant in protecting the rights of citizens, no matter their country of origin.

As early as 1944 *Fortune* magazine warned that the incarceration of Japanese Americans should be a warning to future generations:

> The doctrine of "protective custody" could prove altogether too convenient a weapon in many other situations. In California, a state with a long history of race hatred and vigilantism, antagonism is already building against the Negroes who have come in for war jobs. What is to prevent their removal to jails, to "protect them" from riots? Or Negroes in Detroit, Jews in Boston, Mexicans in Texas? The possibilities of "protective custody" are endless, as the Nazis have amply proved.[125]

As the magazine predicted, discrimination reappeared in the following decades. In the 1950s the government accused thousands of citizens of being sympathetic to the Communist regime in the Soviet Union and arrested numerous citizens for being disloyal to the United States. While some individuals had committed traitorous acts, the vast majority were seen as guilty simply for associating with Communist sympathizers. Discrimination against Mexican Americans started in the 1940s and continues to this day, with the nation involved in a bitter debate over how to close its southern borders to illegal immigrants from Mexico. Japanese Americans know that whenever the American economy sours and that of Japan remains strong, they receive racial slurs and are shunned by some. In the aftermath of the September 11, 2001, terrorist attack on the United States, Arab Americans were labeled as terrorists and mosques were defaced.

The Legacy of Internment

Several organizations have taken steps to make certain the internment is not forgotten and to prevent another such event from occurring in the United States. Dedicated in Washington, D.C., in 2000, the National Japanese American Memorial to Patriotism honors those who were interned and the soldiers who died. The 14-foot (4.3m) bronze sculpture of two cranes, symbolizing happiness, good fortune, and long life, is enmeshed with barbed wire, denoting the camps.

In April 2004 the National Park Service opened an educational center at Manzanar. Exhibits trace the camp's origins and history and prod visitors to compare anti-Japanese bigotry during World War II with twenty-first century anti–Arab American bigotry. Mas Okui, who spent the war years with his family in Manzanar, explained the purpose of the center: "What Manzanar should do is say to people, 'God, we did this. These people were cruelly treated. And I hope it never happens again.'"[126]

Many Japanese Americans experienced additional hardship after the war. Forced to rebuild careers and homes after three years in camp, many were unable to enjoy the same status and economic situation as before the war. People lost homes, possessions, and two

or three years of work at a time when the nation's economy boomed due to the demands of producing war material. Unlike military veterans, who returned to the warm welcome of a grateful nation, Japanese Americans returned to silence.

The internment left a lasting imprint on those who were confined. Manzanar internee Tom Watanabe observed what the government can do to a person it sees as disloyal: "This is supposed to be the people's government, but you as an individual, if they want to fry you they can fry you. It's a frightening thing." He added, "If they put 120,000 of us behind barbed wire without blinking an eye, one guy don't mean nothing."[127]

The sense of betrayal bothered Chiye Tomihiro, who languished in Minidoka. He said, "I remember how we tried to be so patriotic, and we were so trusting. And we used to argue with our parents all the time because we'd say, 'Oh, we're American citizens. Uncle Sam's going to take care of us, don't worry.'" He added, "And to this day I really don't trust this country."[128]

For years after the war Topaz internee Donald Nakahata continued to meet people who, because of his looks, did not consider him an American. Even though Nakahata had been in the country longer than most of his questioners, they marveled that he spoke such fluent English and asked how long he had been in the United States. Nakahata said he got these reactions "because we don't look white American. That's why we have to make it part of the American conscious-

A monument to Japanese Americans is visible behind the barbed wire that borders what is now Manzanar State Historic Park. The National Park Service opened the park, with exhibits, in 2004 to preserve the memory of what happened there.

ness, that you don't have to look like a genuine American to be one."[129]

John Tateishi returned to Manzanar long after he was interned to again look at the grounds and renew memories, and he found that Manzanar was as much a part of him as anything else. He explained, "The experience of America's concentration camps shaped my generation of Japanese Americans, left its indelible mark on all of us, and kept us bound forever to the image of barbed wire and guard towers. No, I thought to myself as I sat there looking at the fading light of Manzanar, no one really ever leaves this place."[130]

Notes

Introduction: Altered Lives

1. James A. Michener. Introduction to *Years of Infamy: The Untold Story of America's Concentration Camps* by Michi Nishiura Weglyn. New York: Morrow, 1976, p. 29.
2. John Y. Tateishi. "Memories from Behind Barbed Wire." In *Last Witnesses: Reflections on the Wartime Internment of Japanese Americans*, edited by Erica Harth. New York: St. Martin's, 2001, p. 129.
3. Tateishi. "Memories from Behind Barbed Wire," p. 129.

Chapter One: Background to Evacuation

4. William C. White. "The Japanese in America: A Close-Up." *New York Times*, January 6, 1935.
5. Quoted in Roger Daniels. *Prisoners Without Trial*. New York: Hill and Wang, 1993, pp. 9–10.
6. Quoted in *New York Times*. "Japan Dispatches a Strong Protest," May 29, 1924.
7. Quoted in Sterling Fisher Jr. "Status of Japanese in America Changes." *New York Times*, September 9, 1934.
8. Quoted in Audrie Girdner and Anne Loftis. *The Great Betrayal*. London: Macmillan, 1969, p. 32.
9. Quoted in Girdner and Loftis. *The Great Betrayal*, p. 7.
10. White. "The Japanese in America," pp. 9, 15.
11. Mary Tsukamoto. "Jerome." In *And Justice for All*, edited by John Tateishi. New York: Random House, 1984, p. 6.
12. Mary Matsuda Gruenewald. *Looking Like the Enemy*. Troutdale, OR: NewSage Press, 2005, pp. 2–4.
13. Quoted in Girdner and Loftis. *The Great Betrayal*, p. 3.
14. Quoted in Girdner and Loftis. *The Great Betrayal*, p. 10.
15. Gruenewald. *Looking Like the Enemy*, p. 5.
16. Wallace Carroll. "Japanese Spies Showed the Way for Raid on Vital Areas in Hawaii." *New York Times*, December 31, 1941.
17. Quoted in Daniels. *Prisoners Without Trial*, p. 38.
18. Quoted in Lawrence E. Davies. "Carrier Is Hunted Off San Francisco." *New York Times*, December 10, 1941.
19. Quoted in Daniels. *Prisoners Without Trial*, p. 28.
20. Quoted in John Morton Blum. *V Was for Victory*. New York: Harcourt Brace Jovanovich, 1976, p. 159.
21. Quoted in John W. Dower. *War Without Mercy: Race and Power in the Pacific War*. New York: Pantheon Books, 1986, p. 81.

22. Quoted in Dower. *War Without Mercy*, p. 80.
23. Quoted in Daniels. *Prisoners Without Trial*, p. 45.
24. Quoted in Tateishi. *And Justice for All*, p. xvi.
25. Quoted in Blum. *V Was for Victory*, p. 158.
26. Quoted in Dower. *War Without Mercy*, p. 92.
27. Quoted in Daniels. *Prisoners Without Trial*, p. 43.
28. Quoted in Lawrence E. Davies. "California Aliens Face Changed Way." *New York Times*, February 5, 1942.

Chapter Two: The Evacuation

29. Quoted in Girdner and Loftis. *The Great Betrayal*, p. 26.
30. Quoted in Girdner and Loftis. *The Great Betrayal*, p. 26.
31. Gruenewald. *Looking Like the Enemy*, pp. 10–11.
32. Quoted in Girdner and Loftis. *The Great Betrayal*, p. 105.
33. Quoted in Blum. *V Was for Victory*, p. 160.
34. Lewis Wood. "Army Gets Power to Move Citizens or Aliens Inland." *New York Times*, February 21, 1942.
35. Gruenewald. *Looking Like the Enemy*, p. 125.
36. Quoted in Girdner and Loftis. *The Great Betrayal*, p. 115.
37. Lawrence E. Davies. "Shifting of Aliens Nearing on Coast." *New York Times*, February 28, 1942.
38. Quoted in Lawrence E. Davies. "Japanese Hurry to Leave Army Zone." *New York Times*, March 29, 1942.
39. Fred Fujikawa. "An Uncertain Future." In *Only What We Could Carry*, edited by Lawson Fusao Inada. Berkeley, CA: Heyday Books, 2000, p. 63.
40. *San Francisco News*. "Their Best Way to Show Loyalty," March 6, 1942. www.sfmuseum.net/hist8/editorial1.html.
41. Eddie Sakamoto. "Manzanar." In *And Justice for All*, p. 17.
42. George Ishida. Letter to the editor. *San Francisco News*, April 13, 1942. www.sfmuseum.net/hist8/editorial6.html.
43. *San Francisco News*. "Bay Area Japs Leaving Coast in Final Rush," March 27, 1942. www.sfmuseum.net/hist8/evac18.html.
44. *San Francisco News*. "Japanese on West Coast Face Wholesale Uprooting," March 4, 1942. www.sfmuseum.net/hist8/intern13.html.
45. Mary Tsukamoto. "Jerome." In *And Justice for All*, p. 9.
46. Tsukamoto. "Jerome." *And Justice for All*, pp. 11–12.
47. Gruenewald. *Looking Like the Enemy*, pp. 26–27.
48. Gruenewald. *Looking Like the Enemy*, pp. 31, 37, 39.
49. Gruenewald. *Looking Like the Enemy*, p. 41.
50. Quoted in Gruenewald. *Looking Like the Enemy*, p. 44.
51. Quoted in United Press. "'Diabolic Savagery,' Tokio Calls Coast Evacuation of Japanese," *San Francisco News*, March 5, 1942. www.sfmuseum.net/hist8/tokio.html.

Chapter Three: Introduction to Camp Life

52. Quoted in Girdner and Loftis. *The Great Betrayal*, p. 155.
53. Mine Okubo. "Citizen 13660." In *Only What We Could Carry*, p. 93.
54. Haruko Niwa. "Manzanar." In *And Justice for All*, p. 29.
55. Marnie Mueller. "A Daughter's Need to Know." In *Last Witnesses: Reflections on the Wartime Internment of Japanese Americans*, p. 103.
56. Quoted in Daniels. *Prisoners Without Trial*, p. 57.
57. Quoted in Daniels. *Prisoners Without Trial*, p. 57.
58. Quoted in Lawrence E. Davies. "Japanese at Work for the U.S." *New York Times*, June 21, 1942.
59. Quoted in Blum. *V Was for Victory*, p. 163.
60. Quoted in Girdner and Loftis. *The Great Betrayal*, p. 259.
61. Jeanne Wakatsuki Houston and James D. Houston. *Farewell to Manzanar*. Boston: Houghton Mifflin, 1973, p. 26.
62. Houston and Houston. *Farewell to Manzanar*, p. 33.
63. Houston and Houston. *Farewell to Manzanar*, p. 27.
64. George Takei. *To the Stars*. New York: Pocket Books, 1994, p. 47.
65. Helen Murao. "Minidoka." In *And Justice for All*, p. 50.

Chapter Four: Daily Life in Camp

66. Quoted in George Takei. "To the Stars." In *Only What We Could Carry*, p. 125.
67. Quoted in National Park Service. "Personal Justice Denied: Report of the Commission on Wartime Relocation and Internment of Civilians," December 1982. www.nps.gov/history/history/online_books/personal_justice_denied/chap6.htm.
68. Gruenewald. *Looking Like the Enemy*, p. 67.
69. National Park Service. "Personal Justice Denied."
70. Eleanor Gerard Sekerak. "A Teacher at Topaz." In *Only What We Could Carry*, p. 131.
71. Sekerak. "A Teacher at Topaz," pp. 132–133.
72. Tsukamoto. "Jerome." In *And Justice for All*, p. 14.
73. Daisuke Kitagawa. *Issei and Nisei: The Internment Years*. New York: Seabury Press, 1967, p. 68.
74. Peter Simpson. "Recollections of Heart Mountain." In *Only What We Could Carry*, pp. 142–148.
75. Simpson. "Recollections of Heart Mountain," pp. 142–148.
76. Simpson. "Recollections of Heart Mountain," pp. 142–148.
77. Simpson. "Recollections of Heart Mountain," pp. 142–148.
78. Houston and Houston. *Farewell to Manzanar*, p. 32.
79. Kitagawa. *Issei and Nisei*, p. 94.
80. Gruenewald. *Looking Like the Enemy*, pp. 72, 151.
81. Quoted in Houston and Houston. *Farewell to Manzanar*, p. 84.
82. Toyo Suyemoto. "Another Spring." In *Last Witnesses: Reflections on the Wartime Internment of Japanese Americans*, p. 34.
83. Guy Gentry. "Absorbing Japs in Normal Life WRA's Problem." *Chicago Daily Tribune*, May 13, 1943.

Chapter Five: Protesting the Internment

84. Paul Shinoda. "Grand Junction, Colorado." In *And Justice for All*, p. 55.
85. Quoted in Tom Watanabe. "Manzanar." In *And Justice for All*, p. 97.
86. Quoted in Peter Irons. *Justice at War*. New York: Oxford University Press, 1983, p. 88.
87. Quoted in Blum. *V Was for Victory*, p. 166.
88. Quoted in Irons. *Justice at War*, p. 99.
89. Quoted in Lewis Wood. "Supreme Court Upholds Return of Loyal Japanese to West Coast." *New York Times*, December 19, 1944.
90. Quoted in Wood. "Supreme Court Upholds Return of Loyal Japanese to West Coast."
91. Quoted in Wood. "Supreme Court Upholds Return of Loyal Japanese to West Coast."
92. Quoted in National Park Service. "Personal Justice Denied."
93. Quoted in Girdner and Loftis. *The Great Betrayal*, p. 275.
94. Quoted in *New York Times*. "Japanese-Americans Will Be Drafted Soon," January 21, 1944.
95. National Park Service. "Personal Justice Denied."
96. Gruenewald. *Looking Like the Enemy*, pp. 119, 123.
97. Houston and Houston. *Farewell to Manzanar*, p. 74.
98. Gruenewald. *Looking Like the Enemy*, p. 118.
99. National Park Service. "Personal Justice Denied."
100. Gruenewald. *Looking Like the Enemy*, p. 132.
101. Quoted in Girdner and Loftis. *The Great Betrayal*, p. 279.
102. Quoted in Girdner and Loftis. *The Great Betrayal*, p. 284.
103. Quoted in *New York Times*. "U.S. Bares Exploits of Nisei in Pacific," October 14, 1945.
104. Quoted in *New York Times*. "Japanese Excel in U.S. Combat Unit," June 6, 1943.
105. Quoted in *New York Times*. "Japanese-Americans Glad to Fight Germans in Italy," October 4, 1943.
106. National Park Service. "Personal Justice Denied."
107. Quoted in *New York Times*. "U.S. Bares Exploits of Nisei in Pacific."
108. Quoted in Girdner and Loftis. *The Great Betrayal*, p. 334.
109. Quoted in *New York Times*. "Nisei Troops Get Truman Citation," July 16, 1946.

Chapter Six: The End of Internment

110. Murao. "Minidoka." In *And Justice for All*, p. 48.
111. Lawrence E. Davies. "Living in America Beckons Evacuees." *New York Times*, May 25, 1943.
112. Quoted in National Park Service. "Personal Justice Denied."
113. *New York Times*. "In the American Tradition," March 7, 1945.
114. *New York Times*. "Internees Hired by Ickes for Farm," April 16, 1943.
115. National Park Service. "Personal Justice Denied."
116. Quoted in *Chicago Daily Tribune*. "Army to Let Japs Go Back to West Coast," December 18, 1944.
117. Quoted in *New York Times*. "Peace Is Welcomed by 33 in Nisei Group." *New York Times*, August 15, 1945.
118. Quoted in Gruenewald. *Looking Like the Enemy*, p. 121.

119. Takei. *To the Stars*, p. 60.
120. Patrick S. Hayashi. "Pictures from Camp." In *Last Witnesses: Reflections on the Wartime Internment of Japanese Americans*, p. 151.
121. Wilson Makabe. "442nd Regimental Combat Team." In *And Justice for All*, p. 259.
122. Quoted in National Park Service. "Personal Justice Denied."
123. Donald Nakahata. "Topaz." In *And Justice for All*, p. 36.
124. Quoted in Lawrence E. Davies. "Citizenship Rights Restored to 2,700." *New York Times*, April 30, 1948.
125. *Fortune*, "Issei, Nisei, Kibei," April 1944, p. 118.
126. Quoted in Sara Song. "The Japanese Camps: Making the 9/11 Link. *Time*, February 16, 2004.
127. Watanabe. "Manzanar." In *And Justice for All*, p. 98.
128. Chiye Tomihiro. "Minidoka." In *And Justice for All*, p. 241.
129. Nakahata. "Topaz." In *And Justice for All*, p. 36.
130. Tateishi. "Memories from Behind Barbed Wire," p. 138.

For More Information

Books

John Morton Blum. *V Was for Victory*. New York: Harcourt Brace Jovanovich, 1976. This account of the home front during World War II contains a concise summary of the Japanese American internment.

Roger Daniels. *Prisoners Without Trial*. New York: Hill and Wang, 1993. This brief account superbly summarizes the wartime internment of Japanese Americans. In clear writing, it describes the steps leading to the evacuations, the court cases, and the redress movement after World War II.

John W. Dower. *War Without Mercy: Race and Power in the Pacific War*. New York: Pantheon Books, 1986. This book, one of the most thoughtful and disturbing books on World War II, shows how racial prejudice against the Japanese affected the nation's political and military policies.

Audrie Girdner and Anne Loftis. *The Great Betrayal*. London: Macmillan, 1969. This is probably the most complete examination of the Japanese American internment. The authors powerfully describe how the relocation to camps disrupted lives and uprooted families.

Mary Matsuda Gruenewald. *Looking Like the Enemy*. Troutdale, OR: NewSage Press, 2005. This is one of the most powerful memoirs to emerge from the Japanese internment. The author, who lived in different internment camps, was a teenager at the time.

Erica Harth, ed. *Last Witnesses*. New York: St. Martin's, 2001. This book offers seventeen essays written by people involved in or affected by the Japanese American incarceration. The powerful pieces examine the incident from differing vantages, providing a complete summation of a difficult time in U.S. history.

Jeanne Wakatsuki Houston and James D. Houston. *Farewell to Manzanar*. Boston: Houghton Mifflin, 1973. One of the first books published about the Japanese internment, *Farewell to Manzanar* is a remarkable, well-written book that offers a powerful account of what life in a camp was like.

Lawson Fusao Inada, ed. *Only What We Could Carry*. Berkeley, CA: Heyday Books, 2000. This book offers firsthand accounts of the internment, as well as poems and cartoons based on the event.

Peter Irons. *Justice at War*. New York: Oxford University Press, 1983. The author of this book is an attorney who was deeply involved in the three important court cases challenging the constitutionality of the relocation and internment of Japanese Americans. He provides his perspective in this thorough account.

Daisuke Kitagawa. *Issei and Nisei: The Internment Years*. New York: Seabury Press, 1967. The author of this book presents a unique view of the Japanese American internment. A minister who worked in the camps, he understood the views of both the Issei and Nisei. This powerful account explains the differing points of view of the two groups and how the internment affected them.

George Takei. *To the Stars*. New York: Pocket Books, 1994. Author George Takei is also an actor, famous for his role as Mr. Sulu in the original *Star Trek* television series and movies. In this book he recounts his family's internment experiences.

John Tateishi, ed. *And Justice for All*. New York: Random House, 1984. Using oral histories from interned Japanese Americans, this book offers moving, first-person accounts that reveal feelings and attitudes of the time.

Michi Nishiura Weglyn. *Years of Infamy: The Untold Story of America's Concentration Camps*. New York: Morrow, 1976. This book provides a clear account of the internment's origins, life in camp, and the effects on people.

Internet Sources

George Ishida. Letter to the editor. *San Francisco News*, April 13, 1942. www .sfmuseum.net/hist8/editorial6.html.

National Park Service. "Personal Justice Denied: Report of the Commission on Wartime Relocation and Internment of Civilians," December 1982. www .nps.gov/history/history/online_ books/personal_justice_denied /index.htm. This government report presents a complete and honest survey of the internment of Japanese Americans.

San Francisco News. "Bay Area Japs Leaving Coast in Final Rush," March 27, 1942. www.sfmuseum.net/hist8/ev ac18.html.

San Francisco News. "Japanese on West Coast Face Wholesale Uprooting," March 4, 1942. www.sfmuseum.net /hist8/intern13.html.

San Francisco News. "Their Best Way to Show Loyalty," March 6, 1942. www .sfmuseum.net/hist8/editorial1.html.

United Press. "'Diabolic Savagery,' Tokio Calls Coast Evacuation of Japanese." *San Francisco News*, March 5, 1942. www.sfmuseum.net/hist8 /tokio.html.

Newspapers

Wallace Carroll. "Japanese Spies Showed the Way for Raid on Vital Areas in Hawaii." *New York Times*, December 31, 1941.

Chicago Daily Tribune. "Army to Let Japs Go Back to West Coast," December 18, 1944.

Lawrence E. Davies. "California Aliens Face Changed Way." *New York Times*, February 5, 1942.

Lawrence E. Davies. "Carrier Is Hunted Off San Francisco." *New York Times*, December 10, 1941.

Lawrence E. Davies. "Citizenship Rights Restored to 2,700." *New York Times,* April 30, 1948.

Lawrence E. Davies. "Japanese Hurry to Leave Army Zone." *New York Times,* March 29, 1942.

Lawrence E. Davies. "Living in America Beckons Evacuees." *New York Times,* May 25, 1943.

Lawrence E. Davies. "Shifting of Aliens Nearing on Coast." *New York Times,* February 28, 1942.

Sterling Fisher Jr. "Status of Japanese in America Changes." *New York Times,* September 9, 1934.

Guy Gentry. "Absorbing Japs in Normal Life WRA's Problem." *Chicago Daily Tribune,* May 13, 1943.

"Internees Hired by Ickes for Farm." *New York Times,* April 16, 1943.

New York Times. "In the American Tradition," March 7, 1945.

New York Times. "Japan Dispatches a Strong Protest," May 29, 1924.

New York Times. "Japanese-Americans Glad to Fight Germans in Italy," October 4, 1943.

New York Times. "Japanese-Americans Will Be Drafted Soon," January 21, 1944.

New York Times. "Japanese Excel in U.S. Combat Unit," June 6, 1943.

New York Times. "Navy Reiterates Ban on U.S. Japanese," August 21, 1944.

New York Times. "Nisei Troops Get Truman Citation," July 16, 1946.

New York Times. "Peace Is Welcomed by 33 in Nisei Group," August 15, 1945.

New York Times. "U.S. Bares Exploits of Nisei in Pacific," October 14, 1945.

William C. White. "The Japanese in America: A Close-Up." *New York Times,* January 6, 1935.

Lewis Wood. "Army Gets Power to Move Citizens or Aliens Inland." *New York Times,* February 21, 1942.

Lewis Wood. "Supreme Court Upholds Return of Loyal Japanese to West Coast." *New York Times,* December 19, 1944.

Periodicals

Fortune. "Issei, Nisei, Kibei," April 1944.

Sara Song. "The Japanese Camps: Making the 9/11 Link." *Time,* February 16, 2004.

Time. "American Fair Play?" March 19, 1945.

Time. "American Scene: Tule Lake 30 Years Later," June 10, 1974.

Time. "It's a Free Country," January 15, 1945.

Time. "Justice: A Different Verdict," February 24, 1986..

Time. "Law: Bad Landmark," November 21, 1983.

Time. "Square Deal for the Japanese," November 29, 1943.

Websites

Densho: The Japanese American Legacy Project (www.densho.org). This site is dedicated to preserving the stories of those who were interned. Its extensive interviews and photographs create a valuable tool for learning about the events leading to and during the internment.

Digital History (www.digitalhistory .uh.edu). This superb site is designed for history teachers and students. It includes official documents, letters, and reports written during and after World War II about the internment of Japanese Americans. It also offers links to other sites.

Smithsonian Education (www.smith sonianeducation.org). This site contains letters written by the residents of the Japanese American internment camps, and thus gives an immediacy that other sources cannot. The site also contains lesson plans for teachers.

Index

Picture Credits

About the Author

John F. Wukovits is a retired junior high school teacher and writer from Trenton, Michigan, who specializes in biographies and history. In addition to writing biographies of Anne Frank, Jim Carrey, Michael J. Fox, Stephen King, and Martin Luther King Jr. for Lucent Books, he has also written biographies of Clifton Sprague, Barry Sanders, Tim Allen, Jack Nicklaus, Vince Lombardi, and Wyatt Earp. He is also the author of many books about World War II, including *Pacific Alamo: The Battle for Wake Island*, *One Square Mile of Hell: The Battle for Tarawa*, *Eisenhower: A Biography*, and *American Commando*. A graduate of the University of Notre Dame, Wukovits is the father of three daughters, Amy, Julie, and Karen, and the grandfather of Matthew, Megan, Emma, and Kaitlyn.